DEPARTMEN

EDUCATIONAL PRIORITY

VOLUME 2: E.P.A. SURVEYS AND STATISTICS

by

JOAN PAYNE

National Research Officer,
Educational Priority Areas Project,
Department of Social and Administrative Studies,
University of Oxford

Report of a research project sponsored by
the Department of Education and Science and
the Social Science Research Council

LONDON
HER MAJESTY'S STATIONERY OFFICE
1974

ISBN 0 11 270296 1

Contents

SECTION A

                                         Page

THE SURVEY OF ATTAINMENT AMONG E.P.A. PUPILS   1

Design of the test programme   1
The tests   3
Bristol Achievement Test scores   5
Immigrant children   6
Overall levels of attainment in the project schools   7
Age and sex differences in vocabulary scores of non-immigrants   ..   14
Age and sex differences in the reading scores of non-immigrant children   19
Attainment of different age groups of immigrant children   21
Correlation between vocabulary and reading scores   23

SECTION B

THE SURVEY OF E.P.A. TEACHERS   24

Design and administration   24
Biographical data   26
Construction and scoring of the attitude scales   31
Relationship between attitudes and biographical data   38
Comparison of the attitudes of E.P.A. teachers with a national sample   42
Job satisfaction of E.P.A. teachers   52
Differences in job satisfaction between project areas   54
Relationship of job satisfaction to age and sex   58
Comparison with job satisfaction in non-E.P.A. samples   60
Relationships among various aspects of job satisfaction   64
Appendix: Questionnaire used in the E.P.A. Project's Survey of Teachers   70

SECTION C

THE SURVEY OF PARENTS   79

Design of the survey   79
The population served by the project schools   82
Pre-school provision and starting school   85
The educational background of the home and ambitions for children ..   86
Helping children at home   88
Contacts between parents and school   89
Children's problems at school and parents' criticisms of the project schools   95
Summary   100
Appendix: Questionnaire used in the Survey of Parents   101

SECTION D   *Page*

PROFILES OF THE PROJECT SCHOOLS   123

SECTION E

STATISTICAL DETAILS OF THE NATIONAL PRE-SCHOOL EXPERIMENT   131

List of Figures

SECTION A

Page

A(1)   Percentage of non-immigrant infants in each project area scoring in various ranges of the E.P.V.T. 1, compared with the corresponding distribution in the nationally representative standardisation sample.   8

A(2)   Percentage of West Indian and Asian immigrant infants in the London and Birmingham project areas scoring in various ranges of the E.P.V.T. 1.   9

A(3)   Percentage of non-immigrant juniors in each project area scoring in various ranges of the E.P.V.T. 2, compared with the corresponding distribution in the nationally representative standardisation sample.   10

A(4)   Percentage of West Indian and Asian immigrant juniors in the London and Birmingham project areas scoring in various ranges of the E.P.V.T. 2.   11

A(5)   Percentage of non-immigrant juniors in each project area scoring in various ranges of the Reading Test S.R.A.   12

A(6)   Percentage of West Indian and Asian immigrant juniors in the London and Birmingham project areas scoring in various ranges of the Reading Test S.R.A.   13

A(7)   Mean E.P.V.T. scores of non-immigrant children, by age and project area.   16

A(8)   Mean E.P.V.T. scores of non-immigrant children, by sex and age.   17

A(9)   Mean E.P.V.T. scores (Level 3) of West Riding secondary modern school children, by year group.   18

A(10) Mean Reading Test S.R.A. scores of non-immigrant children, by sex and age.   20

A(11) Mean E.P.V.T. and Reading Test S.R.A. scores of West Indian and Asian children in the London and Birmingham project schools by age.   22

SECTION B

B(1)   Permissiveness: E.P.A. junior teachers compared with national samples of teachers in streamed and un-streamed junior schools.   44

B(2)   Permissiveness: E.P.A. junior teachers compared with E.P.A. infant teachers.   45

B(3)   Attitudes to physical punishment: E.P.A. junior teachers compared with national samples of teachers in streamed and unstreamed junior schools.   46

B(4)   Attitudes to physical punishment: E.P.A. junior teachers compared with E.P.A. infant teachers.   47

B(5)   Attitudes to noise in the classroom: E.P.A. junior teachers compared with national samples of teachers in streamed and unstreamed junior schools.   48

B(6)   Attitudes to noise in the classroom: E.P.A. junior teachers compared with E.P.A. infant teachers.   49

B(7)   Attitudes to less able children: E.P.A. junior teachers compared with national samples of teachers in streamed and unstreamed junior schools.   50

B(8)   Attitudes to less able children: E.P.A. junior teachers compared with E.P.A. infant teachers.   51

B(9)   E.P.A. teachers' comparisons of their jobs with jobs of friends of approximately the same age and with equivalent qualifications.   52

B(10)   E.P.A. teachers' comparisons of their teaching situation with that of teachers they know in other schools.   53

B(11)   Percentage of teachers in the London project schools who think their teaching situation is worse in various respects than that of teachers they know in other schools, compared with the corresponding percentage of all probationary teachers in primary schools in Southwark.   62

B(12)   Percentage of teachers in the Birmingham project schools who think their teaching situation is worse in various respects than that of teachers they know in other schools, compared with the corresponding percentage of all probationary teachers in primary schools in Wolverhampton.   63

B(13)   Representation in three-dimensional space of the similarities among various aspects of the E.P.A. teachers' satisfaction when comparing themselves with friends in other jobs.   67

B(14)   Representation in three-dimensional space of the similarities among various aspects of the E.P.A. teachers' satisfaction when comparing themselves with teachers in other schools.   68

Section D

D(1)   Profiles of the London project schools.   126

List of Tables

SECTION A

Page

A.1   Schools taking part in the survey of attainment, by size, type and project area.   2

A.2   Percentage of children in project schools tested on the E.P.V.T., by project area.   4

A.3   Children tested on the E.P.V.T. by country of origin and project area.   7

A.4   Children scoring below 80 on the Reading Test S.R.A., by project area and immigrant group.   14

A.5   Mean scores of non-immigrant children aged 7 years 6 months to 7 years 11 months taking different levels of the E.P.V.T.   15

A.6   Comparison of mean reading scores of 8 and 11 year old boys and girls of U.K. and Eire origin in the London E.P.A. project schools with the scores of second and fourth year juniors of U.K. and Eire origin in all London primary schools.   21

A.7   Correlations between E.P.V.T. Level 2 and Reading Test S.R.A. by project area: non-immigrant juniors.   23

SECTION B

B.1   Number of schools taking part in the survey of E.P.A. teachers.   24

B.2   Response rates in the Teacher Survey, by project area and type of school.   25

B.3   Grades of E.P.A. teachers (including unqualified), by project area, compared with all qualified teachers in maintained primary schools in England and Wales at 31st March 1969.   26

B.4   Men and women E.P.A. teachers by project area, compared with all teachers in maintained primary schools in England and Wales at 31st March 1969.   27

B.5   Men and women teachers in E.P.A. infant, junior and junior with infants schools, compared with full-time teachers in all maintained infant, junior and junior with infants schools in England and Wales at January 1969.   27

B.6   Age of E.P.A. teachers (including unqualified) by project area, compared with all qualified teachers in maintained primary schools in England and Wales at 31st March 1969.   28

B.7   Number of years which E.P.A. teachers have spent in the teaching profession, by project area.   28

B.8   Number of years for which teachers have taught in the same school, by project area.   29

B.9   Graduate and non-graduate teachers (including un-qualified) by project area, compared with all qualified teachers in maintained primary schools in England and Wales at 31st March 1969.   30

B.10   Teachers' classifications of their fathers' occupations, by project area.   30

B.11   Distance of teacher's home from school, by project area.   31

B.12   Length of teacher's journey from home to school, by project area.   32

B.13   Guttman attitude scales: comparison of the order of difficulty of items found in the E.P.A. sample with that obtained in the construction samples.   34

B.14   Relationships between attitude scale scores and biographical variables.   40

B.15   Relationship between attitude scale scores and various characteristics of teachers.   41

B.16   Teachers' comparisons of their jobs with the jobs of friends of approximately the same age and with equivalent qualifications, by project area.   56

B.17   Teachers' comparisons of their teaching situation with that of teachers they know in other schools, by project area.   57

B.18   Differences between men and women teachers in the London project schools in their comparisons of their jobs with the jobs of friends of approximately the same age and with equivalent qualifications.   59

B.19   Differences between older and younger teachers in the London project schools in their comparisons of their jobs with the jobs of friends of approximately the same age and with equivalent qualifications.   60

B.20   Matrix of associations (gamma) among E.P.A. teachers' various comparisons of their jobs with the jobs of friends of the same age and with equivalent qualifications.   65

B.21   Matrix of associations (gamma) among E.P.A. teachers' various comparisons of their teaching situation with that of teachers they know in other schools.   66

SECTION C

C.1   Schools taking part in the survey of parents, by type and project area.   80

C.2   Number of interviews achieved in the survey of parents.   80

C.3   Age of selected children in the achieved sample.   81

C.4   Relationship of person interviewed to selected child.   82

C.5   Place where selected child's mother was brought up, by project area.   82

C.6   "Vertical roots" of families in the four project areas.   83

C.7   "Horizontal roots" of families in the four project areas.   84

C.8   Employment of mothers, by project area and family's country of origin.   84

C.9   Number of children in family, by project area and country of origin.   85

C.10   Age mother left school, by project area and country of origin.   87

C.11   Educational background of the home, by project area.   87

C.12   Age at which mothers would like their child to leave school, by project area and country of origin.   88

C.13   Parents' views on the functions of parents and of schools.   89

C.14   Helping children at home, by project area.   90

C.15   Whether parents had a talk with the head when child first went to present school, by project area and country of origin, compared with replies to the same question in the 1964 national survey.   91

C.16   Number of talks parents had had with head or class-teacher, by project area and country of origin, compared with replies to the same question in the 1964 national survey.   92

C.17   Whether husband had visited child's present school or talked to head, by project area and country of origin, compared with replies to the same question in the 1964 national survey.   93

C.18   Parents' attendance at various school activities, by project area and country of origin, compared with the corresponding percentages in the 1964 national survey.   94

C.19   Whether parent knows the name of selected child's headteacher or classteacher, by project area and country of origin.   95

C.20   Attitudes of mothers of families of U.K. and Eire origin towards visiting the school, by project area, compared with the attitudes of mothers in the 1964 national survey.   96

C.21   Whether parents felt their child was getting an education as good as, better, or worse than most children of the same age in Britain, by project area and country of origin.   97

C.22   Changes that parents would like to see in primary schools, by country of origin.   98

C.23   Whether parents thought their child's education was as good as, better, or worse than the education they had at the same age, by project area and country of origin.   98

C.24   Children's problems at school and parents' worries about child's progress, by project area and country of origin.   99

Section D

D.1   Profiles of the project schools in Birmingham, Liverpool and the West Riding.   124

Section E

E.1   Pre-test and post-test scores on the English Picture Vocabulary Test (Pre-school Version) in the national pre-school experiment, by treatment group.   132

E.2   Pre-test and post-test scores on the Expressive Language Scale of the Reynell Developmental Language Scales in the national pre-school experiment, by treatment group.   133

E.3   Pre-test and post-test scores on the Verbal Comprehension Scale of the Reynell Developmental Language Scales in the national pre-school experiment, by treatment group.   134

Preface

This is the second of five volumes reporting our Educational Priority Areas Action-Research Project. It has been written by Mrs. Joan Payne. The first volume, (*E.P.A. Problems and Policies*), which was intended as a general summary account of the project and as a set of recommendations for political, administrative and educational action, appeared in 1972. It had a remarkably attentive and, on the whole, favourable press as well as a response to its proposals concerning the organisation and expansion of nursery education in the Government's White Paper of December 1972[1] and in subsequent developments of the urban programme.

The White Paper was, of course, a general statement of intent covering the whole of the educational system. Much of it, therefore, was of no direct concern to the problems raised in our project. Nevertheless, I suspect that Cmnd. 5174 will come to occupy an important place in the chronology of educational documents because of its reference to nursery education. In effect, Mrs. Thatcher has announced a national intent to form a fourth stage of education, not by mechanical expansion upwards, following post-war trends, but expansion downwards to the under-fives. That way lies new excitement for those who are determined to see education made fully available for all children at all stages no matter what social handicaps attend their birth and background. I think this is the most hopeful road towards educational recreation; a milieu in which family and school can meet and transform the upbringing of their children.

There is, in any case, much to welcome in the White Paper for my E.P.A. colleagues and me. Our cartography of educational deprivation among the under-fives has been incorporated. The signposts of our *Educational Priority*, Volume 1, have become Government properties. We called for a pre-school programme and the Government promises a Plowden level of provision. We asked for positive discrimination and "priority will be given in the early stages of the programme to areas of disadvantage". We wanted local diagnosis and avoidance of standard national formulae and "the Government attaches importance to a full assessment of local resources and needs, and will welcome diversity". We advocated the hybrid vigour of professional nurseries and parent-involved playgroups and the Government will guide and encourage local authorities to equip voluntary groups and provide them with qualified teachers, recognising that "the maturity and experience (of mothers) are important assets" and that "nursery education probably offers the best opportunities for enlisting parental understanding and support for what schools are trying to achieve". We advised further action-research on E.P.A. problems, and this is promised in the White Paper.

Nevertheless, I must also confess to associated doubts and disappointments. First, and probably foremost, is the uncertainty we have as to the fate of our advocacy of the community school. In part this is an uncertainty about what is actually happening. There are indications (in the educational press and in the success of *Priority*, the organisation led by Eric Midwinter

---

[1] Cmnd. 5174.

for the dissemination of E.P.A. ideas) that community school practices have been spreading throughout the country. But there is a need for systematic collection of information which can be readily available to teachers, educational administrators and researchers. Only the D.E.S. could perform this service adequately.

Second, on the pre-school front, there are doubts about the speed and effectiveness of nursery development. To reach Plowden targets by 1981 is to be disappointingly slow. And in the meantime the strength with which the positive discrimination principle is to be applied is very much in doubt. The principle was vaguely put in the White Paper. It should be written in terms of precise measurement and an explicit financial formula. It is not enough to refer hopefully to the experience of the urban programme— though phasing and further grant aid only after inspection would indeed be valuable. The distribution of nursery school resources reported in the press (*Times Educational Supplement, 7.12.73*) do not allay all suspicion that positive discrimination is being given a weak interpretation in practice. I fear that too much has been left by the centre to local discretion.

One theme of doubt (itself an echo of our insistence on the need for local diagnosis) was on the practicability of defining the object of positive discrimination in the geographical terms of the "educational priority area". The present second volume should throw further light on this aspect of E.P.A. problems and serve to underline the necessary sophistication of E.P.A. policies. It does so by offering much more detailed descriptions of E.P.A. conditions than were possible in Volume 1—descriptions based on surveys of E.P.A. pupils, teachers and parents.

During the Project's first year a series of descriptive surveys was carried out covering teachers, parents and pupils in the project schools. Their purpose was both to provide the local project directors with relevant information to help them plan their action strategies, and also to enable the project areas to be compared systematically one with another, thereby indicating why a policy which was successful in one might be inappropriate in another. In so doing, it revealed the disquieting extent of the problems facing the project schools, and how in some schools a number of different problems accumulated. The surveys are briefly described in Chapter 5 of Volume I, where the main results are outlined. In the present volume the design of the surveys is discussed more thoroughly, and the analyses which form the basis of some of the statements made in Volume I are described. We also report some additional analyses which shortage of space had excluded from the first volume. Finally, the volume contains some further statistical details of the Project's national pre-school experiment, an account of which is given in Chapter 7 of Volume 1.

The whole programme of research was agreed and carried out by the research officers attached to each project: in London, Jack Barnes; in Birmingham, Paul Widlake; in Liverpool, Keith Pulham; and in the West Riding, George Smith. Mr. M. A. Brimer, head of the Research Unit in Bristol University Institute of Education, acted as consultant to the research programme and advised on all sections of it. The questionnaire used in the survey of parents was designed by Roger Dale (now of the Open University) and Margaret Davis, and the teacher questionnaire was prepared by Roger Dale and Dr. Terence Lee (now Professor of Psychology at the University of Surrey). Mrs. Payne was not involved in the research programme until the analysis stage, for which she was responsible. Although she wrote the present account, the other research officers helped in many ways with the interpretation of the findings.

The Scottish E.P.A. Project at Dundee also carried out the descriptive surveys under their research officer, Susan Selby. It was originally intended that the Dundee project should publish a separate report, and so the Dundee data was excluded from the cross-project analyses. By the time the decision was made to include an account of the Dundee project in the present series it was too late to add in the Scottish data to the analyses. The reader is hence referred to Volume 5, *E.P.A.: A Scottish Study*, for a description of the Dundee project schools.

We wish to acknowledge the help of Dr. Keith Hope of Nuffield College, Oxford, who wrote the computer programmes which were used for most of the analyses and who gave statistical advice, and of Angela Skrimshire of the Social Evaluation Unit in the Department of Social and Administrative Studies, Oxford University, who also advised on a number of statistical problems and who read and criticised a large part of the manuscript. We are also grateful to Constance Rollett, Pauline Jones and Carol Greene for assistance with coding and the compilation of tables and graphs, and thank the Research Services Unit of Nuffield College, Oxford, for computing help.

A. H. HALSEY
Oxford
10.12.73

The Survey of Attainment among E.P.A. Pupils

Design of the test programme

During the first few months of the E.P.A. Project, the spring and summer terms of 1969, children in the project primary schools were given a series of attainment tests which were designed to answer four questions.

  (i) It was well known that levels of achievement in the project schools were below average, but exactly how great was the gap between them and national standards?

 (ii) There was already evidence from earlier studies that in terms of achievement lower working class children fall further and further behind their contemporaries as they grow older. Did the test scores of E.P.A. children confirm this finding, and could anything be said about the rates of deterioration for children of different ages?

(iii) How did the achievement of immigrant children in the E.P.A. schools compare with that of their non-immigrant classmates, and did they also do progressively worse in relation to national norms as they grew older?

 (iv) Among the basic primary school subjects, were there any in which E.P.A. children did better than others, and any in which their performance was particularly poor?

The analysis of the test scores was able to provide at least partial answers to the first three questions, but, for reasons explained below,[1] we were not able to add any information on the last.

Under the English E.P.A. Project, action-research teams were set up in four areas. Three of these were in run down urban neighbourhoods, including parts of Deptford in South London and inner-ring districts of Birmingham and Liverpool. The fourth—the West Riding project area—comprised two small, economically depressed mining towns in South Yorkshire. The physical characteristics of the project areas and the nature of their populations are described in Chapter 5 of the first volume of this series. All of the project schools in these areas took part in the test programme, with the exception of one junior with infants school and the infant department of another, both in Birmingham. These were left out solely because of the pressure of time, as the Birmingham research officer took up his appointment three months later than the research officers in the other three projects and had only one term in which to complete the whole test programme.

Table A.1 sets out the size and type of the schools in which testing took place. Although there were more schools in Liverpool than any other project area none had more than 300 pupils, and while only six schools were surveyed in Birmingham, they were on average larger than the schools in the other areas. In each area infant and junior schools were fairly evenly balanced: overall there were fifteen separate infant schools, fifteen

---

[1] See page 5.

Table A.1
Schools taking part in the survey of attainment, by size, type and project area

	London			Birmingham			Liverpool			West Riding		
Number of pupils on roll in January 1969:	Infant No.	Junior No.	Junior with infants No.	Infant No.	Junior No.	Junior with infants No.	Infant No.	Junior No.	Junior with infants No.	Infant No.	Junior No.	Junior with infants No.
100–199	1	—	1	—	—	—	4	4	3	4	2	—
200–299	3	1	1	1	—	1*	1	2	2	—	1	1
300–399	1	3	—	—	1	—	—	—	—	—	1	1
400–499	—	—	1	—	—	1	—	—	—	—	—	—
500–599	—	—	—	—	—	1	—	—	—	—	—	—
600–699	—	—	1	—	—	1	—	—	—	—	—	—
Total number of schools	5	4	3	1	1	4	5	6	5	4	4	2

* No tests conducted in the infant department.

junior schools, and fourteen junior with infants schools. The large majority of the schools were maintained by the local authority, but one or two denominational schools in each area were local authority controlled or aided. Two schools only were not co-educational, a boys' and a girls' Roman Catholic junior school in Liverpool.

It was decided to take a complete cross-section of attainment in the schools by testing children in each year group. Clearly some restrictions have to be put on the interpretation of a cross-sectional study, for differences between age groups may be due to the different populations in each age group rather than to changes in individuals as they grow older. A cross-sectional approach was adopted in this case, firstly because test scores were needed at the beginning of the projects to form a baseline of information which would assist in the formulation of action programmes, secondly because there would not have been time in the projects' life spans to follow a single age group for more than three years, and thirdly because the high rates of pupil turnover in many of the schools meant that a follow-up study would be likely to lose large numbers of children over the years. Complete coverage of each year group was attempted as testing random samples of children would have entailed the organisational problems of splitting classes, but shortage of time in Birmingham made it necessary in one infant department to give the individually administered infant vocabulary test to one randomly selected half of the pupils.

The tests

The full test battery included a test of listening vocabulary, a test of reading ability, and tests of attainment in English, mathematics and social and scientific studies. Of these, only the first, the English Picture Vocabulary Test (E.P.V.T.), was appropriate for the full primary school age range. The E.P.V.T. is an anglicised version of the Peabody Picture Vocabulary Test, which has been widely used in the U.S.A. because of the speed and simplicity of its administration. Although it directly measures listening vocabulary, the authors of the E.P.V.T. claim that it can also be used to assess general verbal ability, and they are supported in this by high correlations for a sample of 11-year-olds with tests of verbal ability and English.[1] The E.P.V.T. requires no reading skill, the child's task being to identify, either by pointing or with a mark, one of four pictures which corresponds to a word spoken by the tester. It is intended to be administered by teachers, and the English norms were obtained under those conditions. The test has four levels; of these the Pre-School Version and Level 1 (covering the ages five years to eight years eleven months) are administered individually, while Level 2, which is designed for the ages seven years to eleven years eleven months, and Level 3, for the secondary school age range, are group tests. All levels are standardized on samples of English children at one month intervals to give a mean of 100, a standard deviation of 15, and a range of 60 to 140 points. Standard errors of measurement are estimated at 5·25 points for Level 1 and 4·25 points for Level 2.

Junior classes in the project schools took Level 2 of the E.P.V.T. The test was generally administered by the class teachers under the guidance of the research officers, though in certain special circumstances, such as the

[1] M. A. Brimer and L. M. Dunn, *Manual for the English Picture Vocabulary Tests,* Educational Evaluation Enterprises, 1962. The manual also gives details of the E.P.V.T.'s internal consistency reliability and evidence of its validity.

illness of the class teacher, the research officer himself gave the test. Level 1 was given individually to children in infant classes. Whenever possible the administration was done by members of the research teams, as better conditions could then be achieved than if a teacher had to leave the rest of the class to get on with their work while she tested a child, but the large numbers to be tested meant that many children had nevertheless to be tested by the teacher. 58 children in infant classes in the four project areas were under five at the time of testing: these were given the Pre-School Version of the E.P.V.T.

The total numbers of children in the four project areas for whom we have E.P.V.T. scores are shown in Table A.2. In all nearly nine and a half thousand children were tested, the total being made up of nearly two thousand in Birmingham and the West Riding, just over two and a half thousand in Liverpool, and nearly three thousand in London. Although attempts were made to follow up those who were absent on the first occasion of testing, complete coverage was impossible, and these numbers represented between 86·4 per cent and 93·6 per cent of the numbers on the school roll at January 1969.

Table A.2

Percentage of children in project schools tested on the E.P.V.T., by project area

	London	Birmingham	Liverpool	West Riding
Number tested on E.P.V.T.	2,892	1,990	2,570	1,991
% of total number on project school rolls, January 1969*	88·8%	86·4%†	88·4%	93·6%

* Excluding nursery classes.

† Adjusted for the 50 per cent random sample in one infant department.

These figures are only estimates of the proportion of children who were tested, as numbers on the school rolls fluctuated both between the beginning of the spring term and the start of the testing programme, and also during the course of the testing programme itself. The percentage in Birmingham is low when compared with the percentage of children tested in the other areas because the schools there contained a substantial proportion of immigrant children whose command of English was insufficient to allow them to be tested. The very high proportion of children tested in the West Riding reflects the complete absence of immigrant children in that project area, as well as the lower rates of pupil turnover and absenteeism there.[1]

The reading test which was used was Version A of two parallel tests, Streaming Research A and B (S.R.A. and S.R.B.), developed by the National Foundation for Educational Research for their study of streaming in primary schools.[2] This is a group test covering the junior school age range, which requires children to complete a given sentence with a word chosen from four or five alternatives. In order to perform the task the child must read and understand both the sentences and the alternatives. Like the E.P.V.T., the Reading Test S.R.A. was designed to be administered

---

[1] See Chapter 5 of Volume 1 in this series.

[2] J. C. Barker Lunn, *Streaming in the Primary School,* National Foundation for Educational Research, 1970. Appendix 4 gives details of the test's internal consistency reliability.

by classroom teachers, and is standardized on an English sample at one month intervals to give a mean of 100 and a standard deviation of 15. Its range, however, is slightly narrower, from 70 to 140 points, and its standard error of measurement also slightly smaller, at approximately 3·5 points.[1]

The Reading Test S.R.A. was given to second, third and fourth year juniors in all areas except Birmingham, where shortage of time once more made it impossible to test fourth year juniors. No reading test was given to the younger children. Altogether, 3,815 juniors took the reading test, the area totals being London 1,148, Birmingham 661, Liverpool 1,098 and the West Riding 908. The proportions of children tested in the appropriate age group were similar to those obtained in each area on the E.P.V.T.

The test battery was completed by the Bristol Achievement Tests (B.A.T.), which comprise three separate tests of English, mathematics and "study skills" (the skills used in social and scientific studies), and are suitable for junior school children.[2] All of them require that a child should be able to read if he is to attempt them, and therefore they were given only to those second year juniors and above who had scored 80 or more on the Reading Test S.R.A.

Bristol Achievement Tests scores

It was originally intended that estimated mean scores for full age groups including non-readers would be calculated by using the regression co-efficients of the B.A.T. scores on the Reading Test S.R.A. In normal circumstances this should involve only a slight adjustment to the mean B.A.T. score obtained from the children who were able to read, as only eight or nine per cent of children in each age group would by national standards be expected to obtain reading scores lower than 80. Though it was clear that the proportion of non-readers would be larger in the E.P.A. schools it was not envisaged that they would approach the numbers that were in fact found. The percentage of juniors scoring below 80 on the Reading Test S.R.A. varied from 18 per cent to 36 per cent among children of U.K. and Eire origin in the four project areas, and was even higher for immigrant children. With such large numbers of children excluded from taking the B.A.T., the error involved in estimating mean B.A.T. scores for the full age group was likely to be considerable, especially as the method of estimation involved the questionable assumption that the relationship between the abilities measured by the B.A.T. and the Reading Test S.R.A. was the same for children who could not read as it was for those who could. This assumption was particularly questionable as an examination of the mean reading scores of individual schools suggested that reading skill was related to the methods of teaching used in the school.[3] The formal methods which tended to promote higher attainment in reading did not necessarily also promote high scores on the B.A.T., which had been designed to tap a child's ability to discover answers to questions for himself.

We were left with B.A.T. scores for groups of children from which very variable proportions of non-readers had been excluded, and which were therefore of no use in determining comparative levels of achievement among

---

[1] This information was kindly supplied by Mr. D. A. Pidgeon of the National Foundation for Educational Research.

[2] The tests were designed by M. A. Brimer and associates, and are published by Thomas Nelson and Sons Limited.

[3] For a more complete discussion of this point see Volume 4 of this series.

those groups. No more could the scores be used, as had been intended, to compare the attainment of E.P.A. children in the three basic primary school subjects which the B.A.T. covered, for scores were only available for groups which had been heavily pre-selected for their reading ability. Reading ability is of course more closely correlated with achievement in English than with achievement in mathematics, and one would expect the E.P.A. children taking the B.A.T. to have a higher score in English than in mathematics by reason of their pre-selection alone. Although the scores for individual schools, classes and children (which of course could not be published) were of use both to the schools themselves and to the project teams working with them, it was concluded that it was not worthwhile to undertake a more extensive analysis of achievement as measured by the B.A.T.

Immigrant children

Because of the special problems of children from abroad it was essential in any analysis of the test scores to distinguish immigrant and non-immigrant children. The only uniform way in which this could be done was by the Department of Education and Science's definition of an immigrant child which headteachers use in the Form 7(i) returns from schools each January. The definition excludes children from the Republic of Ireland and children of mixed immigrant and non-immigrant parentage, but includes

(i) children born outside the British Isles who have come to this country with, or to join, parents or guardians whose countries of origin were abroad; and

(ii) children born in the U.K. to parents whose countries of origin were abroad and who came to the U.K. no more than ten years previously.[1]

The definition thus avoids any reference to biological racial characteristics and relies entirely on place of birth and length of parents' residence in this country. There are, however, many children born to parents who have lived in this country for more than ten years who nevertheless have language difficulties or problems of adjustment which call for extra resources on the part of the school. In our own project schools there were, especially in Birmingham, large numbers of children who were not immigrants according to the D.E.S. definition, but who even so came from homes which were linguistically sufficiently diverse as to seriously impair their performance in English schools. This was apparent in the test scores of the "non-immigrant" Birmingham E.P.A. children, which, as will be shown, were well below those of the non-immigrant children in the other three areas.

The problem is complicated by the fact that the D.E.S. definition of an immigrant child, though precise in itself, is often very imprecisely applied, because headteachers do not have the information about parents which it assumes. The fluctuations from year to year in the numbers of immigrant pupils reported to the D.E.S. by some schools give evidence of this. In the E.P.A. Project we were dependent on headteachers to classify children as immigrants or non-immigrants, the numbers involved making it impossible for us to undertake any more direct survey, and our information is inaccurate to the same extent as theirs may have been.

The immigrant groups distinguished among those tested on the E.P.V.T. are shown in Table A.3. There were no immigrants in the West Riding project schools, and very few in Liverpool; on the other hand just under half the pupils in the Birmingham project schools were immigrants according to the D.E.S. definition, as were over a quarter of the children in London.

---

[1] It has been announced that this definition is to be dropped.

In both London and Birmingham there were enough West Indian pupils to form a separate group for analysis, while in Birmingham the Asian group, consisting of Indians and Pakistanis,[1] was also large enough for it to be possible to examine their test scores separately. The "other immigrants" category comprised children of very miscellaneous origins, who were excluded from any general analysis.

Table A.3

Children tested on the E.P.V.T. by country of origin and project area

	London %	Birmingham %	Liverpool %	West Riding %
Non-immigrants (U.K. and Eire)	73·3	56·6	96·2	100·0
Immigrants (D.E.S. definition):				
West Indian	19·0	15·3	—	—
Asian	—	24·8	—	—
Other immigrants and no				
information	7·7*	3·3	3·8†	—
Total %	100·0	100·0	100·0	100·0
(N)	(2,892)	(1,990)	(2,570)	(1,991)

* Including Asian.

† Including West Indian and Asian.

Overall levels of attainment in the project schools

Figure A(1) shows the frequency distributions of scores on Level 1 of the E.P.V.T. for non-immigrant infant school children in each project area. Also given for comparison is the distribution of scores one would expect to find in a nationally representative sample of infant school children, which is based on the scores of 3,240 children in the standardization sample.[2] In all four areas the E.P.A. children did worse than the nationally representative sample, though the difference is smaller in London than elsewhere. The deficit also appears in the mean scores of the E.P.A. children, also given in Figure A(1), which range from two points below the national mean of 100 in London to ten and a half points below in Birmingham. With the exception of London, these low mean scores are due to a general under-representation of the E.P.A. children in the higher scoring categories and a general over-representation in the lower scoring categories, rather than to a single group of very low scoring children. In London the bulk of the children obtained average scores and there was a corresponding deficiency of children falling in the very high score ranges.

The frequency distributions of E.P.V.T. scores for West Indian infant children, shown in Figure A(2), present the same features in an exaggerated form. No West Indian child in the project schools scored more than 114 points, or more than one standard deviation above the national mean, while there were more than twice as many West Indian children in the three bottom score categories as there were in the nationally representative sample. The mean scores were accordingly extremely low: almost one standard deviation below the national mean in London, and well over one standard deviation below in Birmingham.

---

[1] The classification was made before Bangladesh came into existence.

[2] The characteristics of this sample and of the national sample of junior school children mentioned below are described in M. A. Brimer and L. M. Dunn, *op. cit.*

Figure A(1): Percentage of non-immigrant infants in each project area scoring in various ranges of the E.P.V.T. 1, compared with the corresponding distribution in the nationally representative standardization sample.

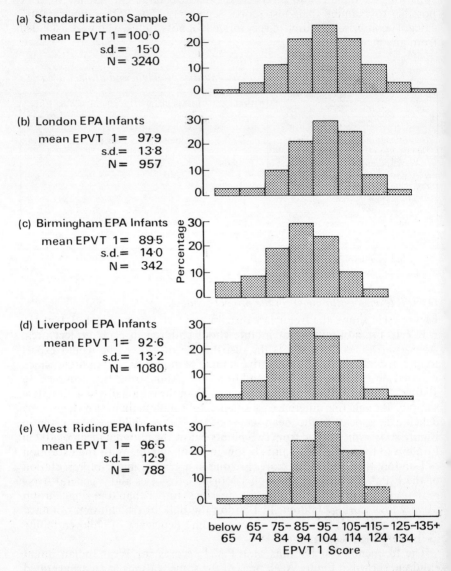

(a) Standardization Sample
    mean EPVT 1=100·0
        s.d.= 15·0
        N = 3240

(b) London EPA Infants
    mean EPVT 1= 97·9
        s.d.= 13·8
        N = 957

(c) Birmingham EPA Infants
    mean EPVT 1= 89·5
        s.d.= 14·0
        N = 342

(d) Liverpool EPA Infants
    mean EPVT 1= 92·6
        s.d.= 13·2
        N = 1080

(e) West Riding EPA Infants
    mean EPVT 1= 96·5
        s.d.= 12·9
        N = 788

below 65- 75- 85- 95- 105-115- 125-135+
  65   74   84   94 104 114 124 134
EPVT 1 Score

The distribution of E.P.V.T. scores of Asian infant children in Birmingham is also given in Figure A(2), and is so strongly skewed as to bear no resemblance to the normal distribution of scores in the nationally representative sample. Ninety per cent of Asian infants scored over one standard deviation below the national mean, and the mean score of the whole group was two standard deviations below. Clearly the E.P.V.T. was in no sense a measure of the general verbal ability of these children, but gave at best an indication of their command of the English language.

Figure A(3) shows the distribution of scores on Level 2 of the E.P.V.T. for non-immigrant junior school children in the four areas, and gives the distribution of scores in a nationally representative sample of junior school children for comparison.[1] In all four areas the mean score of the juniors was lower than the corresponding mean for infants, the difference being five points in London and Liverpool, three points in Birmingham, and two in the West Riding. There is accordingly an increase in the skew of the frequency distributions of the scores, with a higher proportion of children in the lower scoring categories and fewer in the higher scoring ones. With the exception of Liverpool, the modal category—the category in which more scores fall than in any other—is also lower for juniors than for infants. For junior school children the distribution of scores in London has the same basic characteristics as the distributions of scores in the other areas.

The scores of the West Indian junior school children (Figure A(4)) were also lower on average than those of the West Indian infants, though the difference in mean scores—around two points in both London and Birmingham—is not as great as for the non-immigrant children. This may simply be due to a kind of reverse "ceiling" effect: as the scores of the West Indian infants were considerably lower than those of the non-immigrant infants there was less room for further deterioration. The Asian children in Birmingham were the only group in which juniors obtained a higher mean E.P.V.T. score than infants, though the Asians still remained the lowest scoring group among all the juniors. It would be premature to interpret this difference between the infants and the juniors as evidence that the Asian

Figure A(2): Percentage of West Indian and Asian immigrant infants in the London and Birmingham project areas scoring in various ranges of the E.P.V.T. 1.

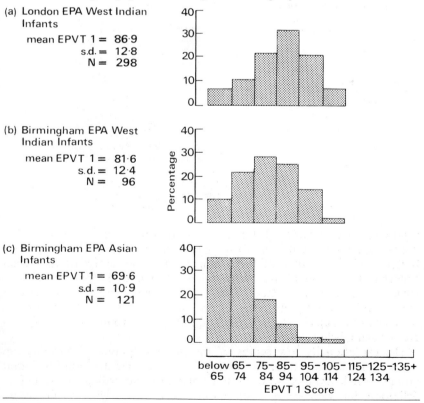

(a) London EPA West Indian Infants

mean EPVT 1 = 86·9
s.d. = 12·8
N = 298

(b) Birmingham EPA West Indian Infants

mean EPVT 1 = 81·6
s.d. = 12·4
N = 96

(c) Birmingham EPA Asian Infants

mean EPVT 1 = 69·6
s.d. = 10·9
N = 121

below 65 / 65–74 / 75–84 / 85–94 / 95–104 / 105–114 / 115–124 / 125–134 / 135+

EPVT 1 Score

[1] See footnote 2 on page 7.

Figure A(3): Percentage of non-immigrant juniors in each project area scoring in various ranges of the E.P.V.T. 2, compared with the corresponding distribution in the nationally representative standardization sample.

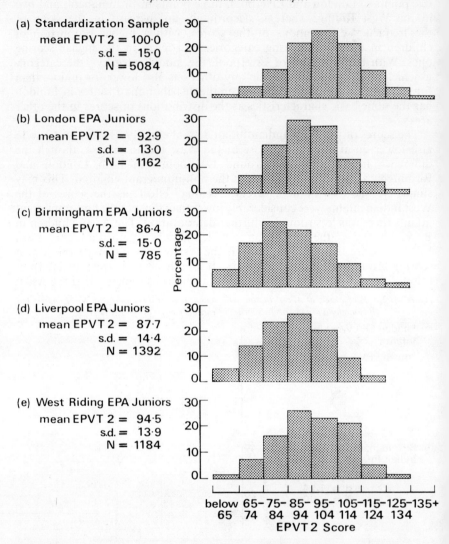

(a) Standardization Sample
    mean EPVT 2 = 100·0
    s.d. =   15·0
    N = 5084

(b) London EPA Juniors
    mean EPVT2 =   92·9
    s.d. =   13·0
    N =   1162

(c) Birmingham EPA Juniors
    mean EPVT 2 =   86·4
    s.d. =   15·0
    N =   785

(d) Liverpool EPA Juniors
    mean EPVT 2 =   87·7
    s.d. =   14·4
    N = 1392

(e) West Riding EPA Juniors
    mean EPVT 2 =   94·5
    s.d. =   13·9
    N = 1184

below 65- 75- 85- 95- 105-115-125-135+
  65 74 84 94 104 114 124 134
            EPVT 2 Score

children's command of English improves as they move through school. The Asian community settled in Birmingham more recently than the West Indian, and at the time of the testing programme newly arrived Asian children of all different ages were being taken into the project schools. Hence a cross-sectional study such as this may merely reflect chance differences between age groups in the proportion of new arrivals. Differences between age groups in all the areas and immigrant groups are discussed in greater detail below.

The exceptionally low scores of the non-immigrants in Birmingham require some comment. As has already been explained, the non-immigrant groups include children who are not immigrants according to the D.E.S. definition, but who are nevertheless of non-British origin. As far as we knew, there were more of such children in Birmingham than in the other

Figure A(4): Percentage of West Indian and Asian immigrant juniors in the London and Birmingham project areas scoring in various ranges of the E.P.V.T. 2.

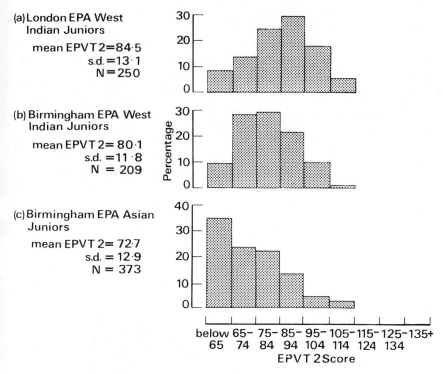

(a) London EPA West Indian Juniors

mean EPVT 2=84·5
s.d.=13·1
N=250

(b) Birmingham EPA West Indian Juniors

mean EPVT 2= 80·1
s.d. =11·8
N = 209

(c) Birmingham EPA Asian Juniors

mean EPVT 2= 72·7
s.d. = 12·9
N = 373

below 65– 75– 85– 95– 105–115–125–135+
    65   74   84   94 104 114 124 134
EPVT 2 Score

E.P.A.s, and it is probable that they depressed the mean score of the non-immigrant group there. Children in the Birmingham project schools also tended to come from larger families than the children in the other three areas,[1] and as there is known to be an inverse correlation between family size and school attainment, this may have been a further factor explaining the lower test scores.

It should also be noted that the West Indian children in Birmingham had lower mean vocabulary scores at both infant and junior level than the West Indian children in the London project schools. We have no means of telling whether this is due to differences between the project schools in the two cities in facilities or methods of teaching, or whether differences in the children's backgrounds are the cause. The latter may well be an important factor, for there are great variations in the type of English spoken by West Indians. Indeed some varieties of English-based Creole are sufficiently different from standard English to be regarded as languages in their own right, and it has been argued that some West Indian children progress better in school if they are taught standard English as though it were a foreign language.[2] The degree to which the language spoken in the home of a West Indian child differs from the language his teachers use will clearly be crucial to his scholastic attainment, especially if his own Creole usages are regarded merely as "sloppy English". Thus for some of the West Indian children the E.P.V.T. may have been functioning as it did for the

---

[1] See Chapter 5 of Volume 1 in this series.
[2] J. Derrick, *Teaching English to Immigrants,* Longmans, 1966.

Asian children, as a test of their command of English rather than of their true vocabulary level or verbal ability.

Figures A(5) and A(6) show the distribution of scores of junior school children on the Reading Test S.R.A. The picture is again one of extremely poor performance, with the majority of children scoring below the national mean. Taking a score of 80 as the point which roughly divides the readers from the non-readers, Table A.4 shows the number of children scoring less than this. In London, Liverpool and the West Riding around a fifth of the non-immigrants tested scored below 80, as did over a third of non-immigrants in Birmingham. Over a quarter of the West Indian children in the London project area and nearly two-fifths in Birmingham were non-readers, while the majority—three-fifths—of Asian children in Birmingham obtained scores indicating an inability to read in English. In contrast, only 8·6 per cent of children in the national sample of junior school children on which the Reading Test S.R.A. was standardized were non-readers. Junior school teachers are generally not taught how to teach reading, for this is thought to be the province of the infant school, yet in the project junior schools a large proportion of children were quite unprepared for the work expected of them.

Figure A(5): Percentage of non-immigrant juniors in each project area scoring in various ranges of the Reading Test S.R.A.

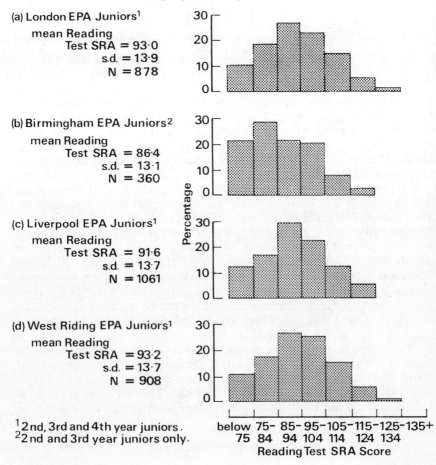

(a) London EPA Juniors[1]

mean Reading
Test SRA = 93·0
s.d. = 13·9
N = 878

(b) Birmingham EPA Juniors[2]

mean Reading
Test SRA = 86·4
s.d. = 13·1
N = 360

(c) Liverpool EPA Juniors[1]

mean Reading
Test SRA = 91·6
s.d. = 13·7
N = 1061

(d) West Riding EPA Juniors[1]

mean Reading
Test SRA = 93·2
s.d. = 13·7
N = 908

[1] 2nd, 3rd and 4th year juniors.
[2] 2nd and 3rd year juniors only.

below 75- 85- 95-105-115-125-135+
75   84   94 104 114 124 134
Reading Test SRA Score

Figure A(6): Percentage of West Indian and Asian immigrant juniors in the London and Birmingham project areas scoring in various ranges of the Reading Test S.R.A.

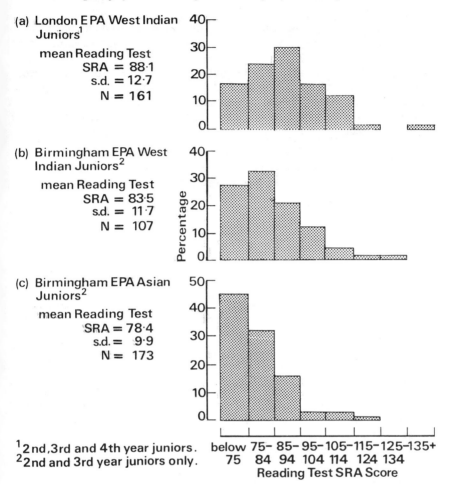

(a) London EPA West Indian Juniors[1]

mean Reading Test
SRA = 88·1
s.d. = 12·7
N = 161

(b) Birmingham EPA West Indian Juniors[2]

mean Reading Test
SRA = 83·5
s.d. = 11·7
N = 107

(c) Birmingham EPA Asian Juniors[2]

mean Reading Test
SRA = 78·4
s.d. = 9·9
N = 173

[1]2nd, 3rd and 4th year juniors.
[2]2nd and 3rd year juniors only.

below 75– 85– 95– 105–115–125–135+
75   84 94 104 114 124 134
Reading Test SRA Score

It is not possible for technical reasons to compare the reading and vocabulary scores directly. It will be recalled that while both the E.P.V.T. and the Reading Test S.R.A. have national means of 100, the latter has a range of only 70 to 140 points compared with the former's range of 60 to 140. In samples of children whose performance is near the national average this would not make much difference, as very few would score at the bottom of the range. However we have already seen that a substantial proportion of the E.P.A. children fall in the bottom score categories of both tests. It follows that their scores on the Reading Test S.R.A. will tend to be higher than their scores on the E.P.V.T., simply because on the reading test it is not possible to score below 70.

Clearly, as the test programme was conducted in schools in four more or less arbitrarily chosen areas it is not possible to generalise from the results to any very accurate statement about the levels of attainment that might be found in E.P.A. schools throughout the country. The variations among the four areas studied suggest that still wider variations could occur nationally among schools in similar areas. Nevertheless, the scores have a greater interest than merely that of the record of particular schools in particular underprivileged areas. Every one of the education authorities taking part in the E.P.A. project could have named many other schools which were equally badly off as those selected for study. Hence the fact that in the project schools in all four areas levels of attainment, though variable, were alike in being extremely low by national standards is itself of disturbing significance. When nationally representative samples of schools are studied, schools like those taking part in the E.P.A. Project must necessarily appear only as isolated extremes, and it is easy to overlook the enormity of the task of raising attainment in the E.P.A. schools to standards considered normal elsewhere.

Table A.4

Children scoring below 80 on the Reading Test S.R.A., by project area and immigrant group

| | Non-immigrants (U.K. and Eire) | | | |
	London	Birmingham	Liverpool	West Riding
Number tested	878	360	1,061	908
% scoring below 80	19·0%	35·8%	21·7%	17·7%

| | | Immigrants | |
	West Indians (London)	West Indians (Birmingham)	Asians (Birmingham)
Number tested	161	107	173
% scoring below 80	26·7%	39·2%	60·1%

Age and sex differences in vocabulary scores of non-immigrants

One of the purposes of the survey of attainment in project schools was to compare the performance of E.P.A. children of different ages. The research carried out for the Coleman Report in the U.S.A. had shown that the difference between the average verbal ability of whites and of blacks in rural areas of the south and southwest was greater in the higher than in the lower school grades.[1] This was an important finding, for it suggested that the schools themselves may be instrumental in widening the gap between privileged and under-privileged groups. In this country, the follow-up study of a random national sample of 5,000 children conducted by Douglas and his colleagues established that the attainment of lower working class children in vocabulary and reading deteriorated in relation to national standards between the ages of eight and eleven, and that no improvement had taken place when the children were re-tested at fifteen years.[2] If, then, E.P.A. children leave school worse off in relation to their more fortunate contemporaries than they were when they started, there is serious cause for concern.

Unlike the Coleman and Douglas studies the E.P.A. testing programme did not allow comparisons to be made between children in E.P.A. schools and children in more advantaged situations. However both the E.P.V.T. and the Reading Test S.R.A. are standardized so that for each age group

---

[1] J. S. Coleman *et al., Equality of Educational Opportunity,* U.S. Department of Health, Education and Welfare, 1966.

[2] J. W. B. Douglas, J. M. Ross and H. R. Simpson, *All Our Future,* Peter Davies, London, 1968.

the mean score of a nationally representative sample of children is 100. We were thus able to examine how far E.P.A. children fell below the national mean at different ages.

Of the two tests only the E.P.V.T. covered the full primary school age range: Level 1, which is individually administered, is designed for infant school children, and Level 2, which is group administered, is designed for juniors. The question therefore arises of whether it is meaningful to compare the scores of infants with the scores of juniors, or whether comparisons can only be made within the age range appropriate to each level of the test. As the two age ranges overlap, it was possible to test whether the two levels gave equivalent results for children of the same age. It was obviously more convenient to give all children in the same class the same level of the E.P.V.T., and the variations between schools in the way that children of different ages were grouped into classes meant that in London and Liverpool non-immigrant pupils aged seven years six months to seven years eleven months were split sufficiently evenly between Levels 1 and 2 to allow the mean scores on each level to be compared. The results are set out in Table A.5. In both areas the difference between the two means— 0·8 points in London and 0·1 points in Liverpool—was negligible. This was confirmed by a comparison of the mean scores of non-immigrant children in adjacent six month age groups in Birmingham and the West Riding, where the younger group was tested on Level 1 and the older on Level 2. In both cases the difference between the mean scores of the two groups was very small, being only 0·4 points in Birmingham and 0·1 points in the West Riding. We therefore felt justified in treating the two versions of the E.P.V.T. as equivalent for the purpose of comparisons among different age groups.

Table A.5

Mean scores of non-immigrant children aged 7 years 6 months to 7 years 11 months taking different levels of the E.P.V.T.

	London		Liverpool	
	No.	Mean score	No.	Mean score
E.P.V.T. Level 1	65	94·6	63	89·1
E.P.V.T. Level 2	127	93·8	99	89·0

Figure A(7) graphs the mean score of each one-year age group from five plus to eleven plus in each area and also gives the number of children on which each point in the graph is based. The smallest age group in any area contains over a hundred children, and the median group size is around 300. The relationship between vocabulary score and age, taking children of U.K. and Eire origin only, proved to be remarkably similar in all four areas. It has three main features. During the first year at infant school scores remain fairly steady or even improve slightly. However between the ages of six and seven a fall occurs, which continues in the West Riding until the children are over eight years old, and in the other areas until they are over nine. At this point scores begin to rise again, and the gains made in one year are held fairly steadily until the end of the primary school. The gains are not great enough, however, to prevent the eleven-year-olds about to leave primary school from performing worse in relation to the national average than the five-year-olds in the reception classes.

Figure A(7): Mean E.P.V.T. scores of non-immigrant children, by age and project area.

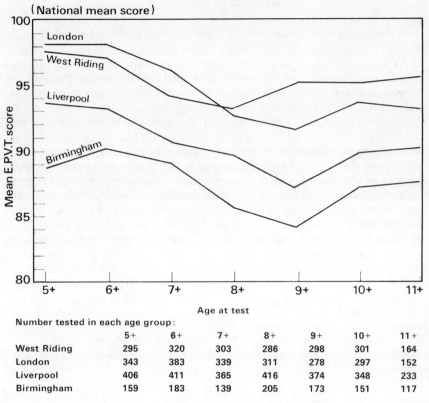

Number tested in each age group:

	5+	6+	7+	8+	9+	10+	11+
West Riding	295	320	303	286	298	301	164
London	343	383	339	311	278	297	152
Liverpool	406	411	365	416	374	348	233
Birmingham	159	183	139	205	173	151	117

When separate curves were plotted for each sex, as in Figure A(8), it was obvious that the boys performed consistently better on the E.P.V.T. than the girls. This sex difference was also found in the standardization sample of the test, and indeed seems to be generally true of orally administered vocabulary tests.[1] Figure A(8) also suggests that the boys' superiority is greater on Level 2 than Level 1, and although the authors of the test do not remark on this in the test manual their own figures for the standardization sample appear to confirm this tendency.

Despite the differential effect of sex, the main features of the relationship between score and age were preserved in the separate curves for boys and girls in all of the project areas except the West Riding, where the pattern appeared to break down. It is probable therefore that the similarity between the West Riding and the other areas apparent in Figure A(7) was purely coincidental. The consistency of the relationship between age and score in the three inner city E.P.A.s is, however, remarkable, and it would be reasonable to infer that it reflects processes which hold true for non-immigrant children in deprived inner city schools generally.

We cannot say with any certainty what these processes are, but we can make some informed speculations. The curves are derived from a cross-sectional study and therefore their interpretation is less clear than if the same group of children had been followed throughout their primary school career. In particular, it opens the possibility that the overall decline in score

[1] M. A. Brimer and L. M. Dunn, *op. cit.,* p. 30.

is due to selective migration out of the project areas by the more able families. It is conceivable that such migration contributes something to the decline, but as the main explanation it is implausible. The three inner city areas cover very different types of housing: from partially demolished terraces to new estates of high rise council flats. The Birmingham project area contained a substantial immigrant population while in Liverpool the number of immigrants was small. With such varied housing markets in the three areas it is most unlikely that selective out-migration would lead to the very similar slopes and shapes of the curves which we see in Figure A(7). It is also unlikely that out-migration would lead to a decline in mean test score as great as that which occurred between children aged five and nine years. We therefore base our interpretation of the differences between the mean test scores of different age groups on the assumption that they reflect real changes in the performance of children as they grow older, rather than differences in the composition of the age groups.

Figure A(8): Mean E.P.V.T. scores of non-immigrant children, by sex and age.

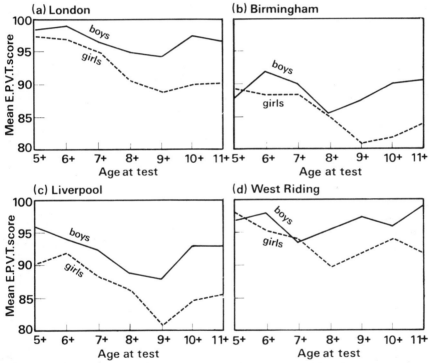

The relative steadiness of test score between five and six years could then be explained by the novelty of the first year at school, which often seems to be stimulating to underprivileged children. As the novelty wears off less favourable attitudes set in, and the decline in test score between the ages of six and nine may be due partly to this. The situation may be worsened by the fact that in many primary schools the middle years are not seen to be as critical as the later ones, and it is common practice for the least experienced teachers to be allocated to the bottom juniors. During the third and fourth year juniors instruction becomes more intensive as children are prepared for eleven plus selection and transfer to secondary school—it is often here that the best teaching resources of the junior school are concentrated. The upswing in scores between the ages of nine and eleven quite possibly could be a product of this extra effort.

This pattern of decline and recovery cannot be equally marked for all primary school children, both privileged and underprivileged, for then the standardization of the E.P.V.T. would make it undetectable in the E.P.A. schools. We may indeed hypothesize that it is characteristic of schools where teaching resources are limited and where as a result priorities have to be established for the allocation of resources. This hypothesis is supported by the fact that in the West Riding there appeared to be no consistent relationship between test score and age when scores were broken down by sex, for teacher turnover there was considerably less than in the three inner

Figure A(9): Mean E.P.V.T. scores (Level 3) of West Riding secondary modern school children, by year group.

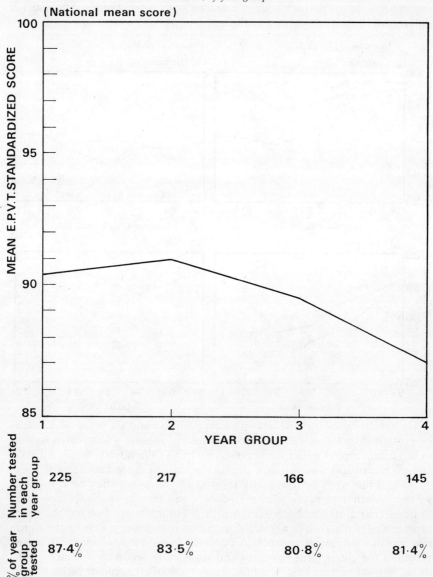

city areas. Half of the teachers in the West Riding project schools had taught in the same school for five years or more, compared with a quarter in the London and Birmingham schools, and the average age of teachers was much greater.[1] We would expect therefore that because a higher proportion of the teachers were experienced, there would not be the same contrast between the bottom and top juniors in the West Riding schools as in the inner cities.

If the interpretation argued in the preceding paragraphs is correct, it has important implications for educationalists. On the one hand it corroborates the finding of the Coleman Report that underprivileged children show a "cumulative deficit" in educational performance as they grow older, but on the other it suggests that this deficit is not due solely to factors beyond the school's control, be they social or genetic. On the contrary, it seems that the decline in performance can be reversed simply by intensive teaching.

In the West Riding project area, children at the local secondary modern school were also tested on the E.P.V.T., using Level 3 of the test. The whole of this school's intake came from the project primary schools, of which it took roughly 85 per cent of the junior school leavers. Of the rest, 10 per cent went to selective schools and 5 per cent to other non-selective schools. Like the West Riding primary schools, the secondary modern had no immigrant pupils. Figure A(9) shows the mean test scores achieved by the first, second, third and fourth year pupils, with the numbers and percentage of year group on which each mean is based. The mean score of the first formers was 90·5, some five points below that of the eleven year olds in the junior schools, and due no doubt to the transfer of the cleverest children to grammar school. The second formers had an almost identical mean score, but during the third and fourth years there was a progressive fall and the mean score of the children in their final year was three and a half points below that of the new entrants. In each year group quite a lot of children were absent for the test. However one would expect the absentees to have on average a lower score than those who were present, as the latter should include a higher proportion of regular attenders. Thus the exclusion of the absentees, of whom there were more in the older than in the younger year groups, probably lessens the apparent decline.

Obviously general conclusions cannot be drawn from tests in a single school. However many teachers would be not in the least surprised by these scores, as increasing apathy and truancy as fourteen and fifteen year olds mark time before starting work is a phenomenon with which they are all too familiar.

Age and sex differences in the reading scores of non-immigrant children

Figure A(10) plots scores on the Reading Test S.R.A. by sex and age. Unlike the E.P.V.T., no clear relationship between reading score and age can be discerned which is constant for each sex across all four project areas. This is partly, though by no means entirely, because the age span of the children tested is much narrower, and because in Birmingham no scores were obtained for the eleven plus age group.

A good deal of consistency can however be observed in the differences between the sexes. In each area the girls score higher than the boys at the

---

[1] See page 28 below.

age of eight years: in the West Riding they have an advantage of one
point and in the other three areas of a full three points. However in the
oldest age groups tested the boys have caught up some of this leeway,
and in Liverpool they have even overtaken the girls. In this pattern the
E.P.A. children's scores closely reflect the sex differences found in other
studies of reading attainment.

Figure A(10): Mean Reading Test S.R.A. scores of non-immigrant children, by sex and age.

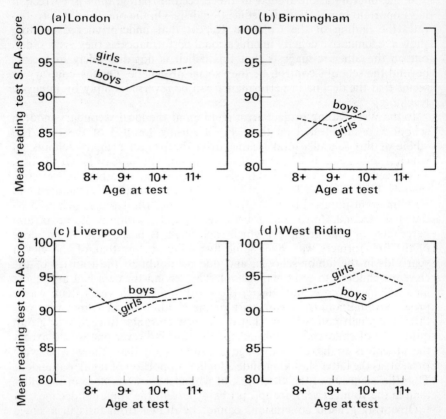

In 1968 the Inner London Education Authority conducted a survey of
reading attainment among second year juniors in all London primary
schools, using the same test that was used in the E.P.A. studies, the Reading
Test S.R.A. Three years later the same cohort, now in the top juniors, was
tested a second time on the parallel form of the test, the Reading Test
S.R.B.[1] In all, 31,308 children including both immigrants and non-
immigrants were tested in 1968 and 31,731 in 1971, though only 26,202
took part in both surveys. In Table A.6 we show how the mean reading
scores for boys and girls of U.K. and Eire origin in all London primary
schools differ from the mean reading scores of children of the same origins
in comparable age groups in the E.P.A. project schools in London.[2]

---

[1] Results of the two surveys are reported in *Literacy Survey: 1971 Follow-up—Preliminary
Report*, I.L.E.A. Research and Statistics Group, 1972, and in an internally circulated paper,
I.L.E.A. Literacy Survey: Sex Differences.

[2] We are grateful to Dr. M. D. Shipman, Director of the I.L.E.A. Research and Statistics
Group, for making these figures available.

Table A.6

Comparison of mean reading scores of eight and eleven year old boys and girls of U.K. and Eire origin in the London E.P.A. project schools with the scores of second and fourth year juniors of U.K. and Eire origin in all London primary schools

	Boys			Girls		
	N	Mean	S.d.	N	Mean	S.d.
London E.P.A. project schools:						
8y. 0m. to 8y. 11m. (S.R.A.)	68	92·4	15·1	71	95·3	14·5
11y. 0m. to 11y. 11m. (S.R.A.)	72	91·8	11·7	78	94·2	12·7
*All London primary schools**						
Second year juniors (S.R.A.)	13,235	94·4	15·4	12,862	97·5	13·9
Fourth year juniors (S.R.B.)	10,949	95·9	16·6	10,649	96·3	14·5

* *Source:* I.L.E.A. Literacy Survey.

The I.L.E.A. figures confirmed the trend in sex differences which we found in the E.P.A. schools, with a large difference in favour of girls in the second year juniors being substantially narrowed by the end of the junior school. However there are other important comparisons between the two sets of means. In each age group and for each sex, the E.P.A. children gained, as expected, a mean score lower than the mean for all London primary school children, and the difference was quite large, ranging from 2·0 points to 5·1 points. Furthermore, both boys and girls among the E.P.A. eleven year olds had a lower mean score than eight year olds of the same sex, while taking boys and girls together there was a slight overall increase in mean score between the second and fourth year juniors in all London primary schools. Obviously the comparison between the I.L.E.A. and the E.P.A. figures is rough, for the one was a follow-up and the other a cross-sectional study and different versions of the reading test were used in the older age group. It does nonetheless support the evidence of the mean standardized E.P.V.T. scores shown in Figure A(7) that E.P.A. children fall progressively further behind their age-mates as they grow older.

Attainment of different age groups of immigrant children

Figure A(11) shows the mean vocabulary and reading scores of different age groups of West Indian children in the London project schools, and of West Indian and Asian children in Birmingham. Numbers were not large enough to control for sex, but the relationship between mean E.P.V.T. score and age group was very similar for West Indian children in both areas. When small numbers are involved fluctuations are to be expected, so this consistency is remarkable. In each area, scores increased between the five and seven year old groups, but dropped sharply between seven and ten. Only after that point did the two groups diverge, the scores of the Birmingham children rising while those of the London children fell still further. Comparing these curves with the equivalent curves for non-immigrant children in Figure A(7), it appears that the test scores of West Indian E.P.A. children begin to fall off earlier than the scores of their non-immigrant classmates, and that the decline continues for longer. This difference could of course be a peculiar feature of the particular schools taking part in the E.P.A. Project, but the striking similarity between the age curves in the two different project areas suggests that they reflect more general patterns in the performance of West Indian children.

Figure A(11): Mean E.P.V.T. and Reading Test S.R.A. scores of West Indian and Asian children in the London and Birmingham project schools by age.

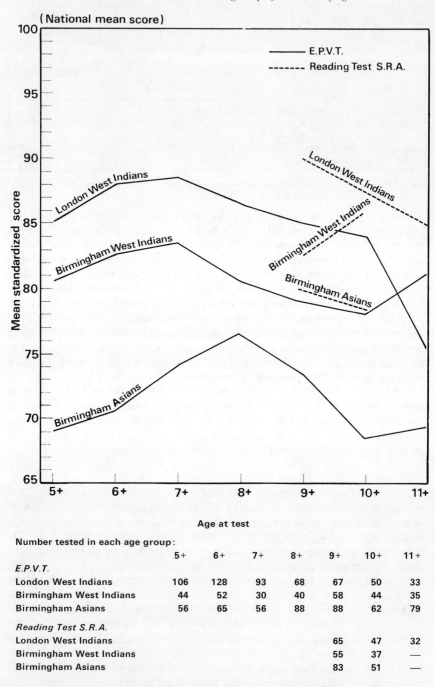

Number tested in each age group:

	5+	6+	7+	8+	9+	10+	11+
E.P.V.T.							
London West Indians	106	128	93	68	67	50	33
Birmingham West Indians	44	52	30	40	58	44	35
Birmingham Asians	56	65	56	88	88	62	79
Reading Test S.R.A.							
London West Indians					65	47	32
Birmingham West Indians					55	37	—
Birmingham Asians					83	51	—

The numbers of West Indian children taking the Reading Test S.R.A. permitted only a very limited comparison of the reading ability of different age groups, and, as for the non-immigrants, no consistent pattern was found across the two areas. In the London West Indian group standardized reading scores, like vocabulary scores, declined steeply between nine and eleven years, while the Birmingham group showed an increase in score between the nine and ten year olds, the only two age groups for which sufficient numbers were available. The I.L.E.A. Literacy Survey however also found a decline in reading standards among West Indian pupils during the course of the junior school: the second year juniors tested had a mean score on the Reading Test S.R.A. of 87 points, compared with a mean score for the top juniors of 85 points.

The Asian community is on the whole not so long established in this country as the West Indian, and a number of Asian children enter infant or junior classes directly from abroad. Hence a cross-sectional study like the E.P.A. study may mislead if interpreted as showing the progress of Asian children through school, for different age groups may contain different proportions of new arrivals. Nevertheless the curve of mean E.P.V.T. scores for separate age groups of Asian children has some similarities with the curves for West Indian children. Their scores also improved steadily throughout the infant school, but the improvement continued for one year longer, until the eight plus age group. From this point onwards there was a rapid decline, with a slight upswing, like the West Indian children in Birmingham, in the last year of junior school. Their reading scores, which were only measured between nine plus and ten plus, paralleled the decline in vocabulary scores between these ages.

Correlation between vocabulary and reading scores

Correlations between Level 2 of the E.P.V.T. and the Reading Test S.R.A. are shown in Table A.7, from which immigrants are excluded. The correlations are very consistent across the four areas, ranging only from ·557 to ·603. The authors of the E.P.V.T. report a rather stronger relationship between the E.P.V.T. and tests of reading ability: in a sample of 223 children aged eight to eleven years in an urban primary school they found a correlation of ·80 between E.P.V.T. 2 and the Schonell Graded Word Reading Test, and in a further sample of 124 children aged ten years nine months to eleven years three months there was a correlation of ·706 between E.P.V.T. 2 and the Vernon Graded Word Reading Test. The lower correlation of the Reading Test S.R.A. with the E.P.V.T. may well be because it is a different type of test from the graded word reading tests. The latter require the child to pronounce correctly a list of separate words, while the Reading Test S.R.A. demands that he read complete sentences and put in a missing word from an understanding of the context.

Table A.7

Correlations between E.P.V.T. Level 2 and Reading Test S.R.A. by project area: non-immigrant juniors*

	London	Birmingham	Liverpool	West Riding
Pearson's r	·557	·574	·583	·603
No. of children	809	331	988	902

* Excluding first year juniors in all project areas and fourth year juniors in Birmingham.

The Survey of E.P.A. Teachers

Design and administration

The Teacher Survey was designed to collect information from all teachers in the E.P.A. project schools on their backgrounds and careers, attitudes to various aspects of teaching, and job satisfaction. On each of these subjects some comparative data for teachers in non-E.P.A. schools was available. The sections of the questionnaire on career history and job satisfaction were designed by Roger Dale, who acted as a consultant to the E.P.A. Project from Bristol University Institute of Education. Dr. Terence Lee, who was then a member of the Department of Psychology at Dundee University and supervised research in the Dundee E.P.A. Project,[1] selected the attitude scales, which included three scales specially constructed by him. A copy of the questionnaire is given in the Appendix to this section.

The questionnaire was cleared by the teachers' unions and by the relevant local education officers and teachers' organisations. It was distributed via headmasters to teachers in the schools listed in Table B.1 in the summer term of 1969, and completed questionnaires were either collected by the heads or returned directly by post. Response rates are set out in Table B.2. In London, Birmingham and the West Riding they were better than usual for a postal survey, with an overall response rate of 79 per cent. However in Liverpool returns were very low indeed on account of objections by some schools to the questions, and because of this Liverpool teachers were excluded from many of the analyses. Table B.2 also shows that response rates tended to be better in infant schools than in junior or junior with infants schools, and hence infant teachers are slightly over-represented in the survey.

Table B.1

Number of schools taking part in the survey of E.P.A. teachers

Type of school	London N	Birmingham N	West Riding N	London, Birmingham and West Riding total N	Liverpool N
Nursery	1	0	0	1	0
Infant	5	1	4	10	4
Junior with infants	3	5	2	10	3
Junior	4	1	4	9	5
Total	13	7	10	30	12

[1] For reasons explained in the Preface data from the Dundee Project is not included in the analyses in this volume.

Table B.2
Response rates in the Teacher Survey, by project area and type of school

Type of school	London E.P.A.			Birmingham E.P.A.			West Riding E.P.A.			London, Birmingham and West Riding total			Liverpool E.P.A.		
	No. questionnaires sent out	returned	% response	No. questionnaires sent out	returned	% response	No. questionnaires sent out	returned	% response	No. questionnaires sent out	returned	% response	No. questionnaires sent out	returned	% response
Nursery	8	7	86%	0	—	—	0	—	—	8	7	86%	0	—	—
Infant	58	51	88%	8	7	86%	19	17	89%	85	75	88%	21	10	48%
Junior with infants	44	35	80%	79	54	68%	22	20	91%	145	109	75%	23	4	17%
Junior	67	50	75%	11	9	82%	30	22	73%	108	81	75%	36	14	39%
Type of school not identified	—	2	—	—	0	—	—	0	—	—	2	—	—	0	—
Total	177	145	82%	98	70	71%	71	59	83%	346	274	79%	80	28	35%

Biographical data

In order to build up a picture of the type of staff in E.P.A. schools the survey included questions on basic personal details and career histories. As the comparison made in Table B.3 suggests, the proportions of teachers in the survey holding various posts were very similar to the proportions in all ᐧ

Table B.3

Grades of E.P.A. teachers (including unqualified), by project area, compared with all qualified teachers in maintained primary schools in England and Wales at 31st March 1969

Grade	London E.P.A. %	Birmingham E.P.A. %	West Riding E.P.A. %	London, Birmingham and West Riding total %	All England and Wales* %
Heads	10	7	14	10	15
Deputy heads, heads of department, and 2nd masters/ mistresses	9	19	12	12	12
Graded posts	9	14	5	9	9
Other assistants	67	59	63	64	63
No information	6	1	7	5	0
Total %	100	100	100	100	100
(N)	(145)	(70)	(59)	(274)	(153,259)

* Source *Statistics of Education 1969*, Vol. 4, Table 21 (H.M.S.O. 1971). The figures for England and Wales include nursery schools, all-age schools and visiting and relief teachers in primary schools.

maintained primary schools in England and Wales. There were some variations among areas, due to the different numbers and types of schools in each: obviously there would be fewer heads and more departmental heads or graded posts in Birmingham, where the project schools were mostly large junior with infants schools, than in London or the West Riding, where the majority were separate infant or junior schools. The ratio of men to women among the E.P.A. teachers surveyed was identical with the ratio for the whole of England and Wales (see Table B.4), though again there were variations among project areas, the London and West Riding schools having slightly fewer men teachers than the national average and the Birmingham schools rather more. Table B.5 shows further that the proportions of men and women teachers were broadly the same as the national average within infant, junior and junior with infants schools taken separately.

Despite the similarity in these basic respects between the E.P.A. teachers surveyed and primary school teachers nationally, teachers in the London and Birmingham E.P.A.s were considerably younger than their fellow teachers in the rest of England and Wales. In Table B.6 we see that 18 per cent of teachers in maintained primary schools in England and Wales were under 25 in 1969, compared with 32 per cent in the London project schools and 27 per cent in Birmingham. At the other end of the age scale, 28 per cent of teachers in London and 20 per cent in Birmingham were

Table B.4

Men and women E.P.A. teachers by project area, compared with all teachers in maintained primary schools in England and Wales at 31st March 1969.

	London E.P.A. %	Birmingham E.P.A. %	West Riding E.P.A. %	London, Birmingham and West Riding total %	All England and Wales* %
Men	22	37	22	26	26
Women	78	63	78	74	74
No information	1	0	0	0	0
Total %	100	100	100	100	100
(N)	(145)	(70)	(59)	(274)	(155,588)†

* Source *Statistics of Education 1969*, Vol. 4, Table 15. Includes nursery schools, all-age schools and visiting and relief teachers in primary schools.

† Refers to *all* teachers in maintained primary schools in England and Wales, while the corresponding figure in Table B.3 refers only to all *qualified* teachers.

Table B.5

Men and women teachers in E.P.A. infant, junior and junior with infants schools, compared with full-time teachers in all maintained infant, junior and junior with infants schools in England and Wales at January 1969

	London, Birmingham and West Riding E.P.A.s*			All England and Wales†		
	Infant schools %	Junior with infants schools %	Junior schools %	Infant schools %	Junior with infants schools %	Junior schools %
Men	3	31	42	0	27	40
Women	97	68	58	100	73	60
No information	0	1	0	0	0	0
Total %	100	100	100	100	100	100
(N)	(75)	(109)	(81)	(37,143)	(74,648)	(49,458)

* The 9 teachers at the London nursery school surveyed are excluded.

† Source *Statistics of Education 1969*, Vol. 1, Table 14. The total number of teachers is different from that given in Table B.4 which is derived from Table 15 in Vol. 4. According to the "Explanatory Notes" to Vol. 4 (paragraph 29), "The statistics in Tables 15 to 42 (in Vol. 4) are derived from an analysis of the Department's salary and superannuation records. The statistics of full-time teachers in schools given in *Statistics of Education 1969, Volume 1* are derived from a different source, namely returns submitted by individual schools in January each year and are not comparable in all respects with those given in this Volume."

45 or older, compared with a national figure of 36 per cent. The contrast between the West Riding project schools and the others is striking in this respect, for the West Riding teachers were about as far above the average age for primary school teachers nationally as the London and Birmingham teachers were below it. Only 10 per cent of teachers there were under 25, and 46 per cent were 45 or more.

Table B.6

*Age of E.P.A. teachers (including unqualified) by project area, compared
with all qualified teachers in maintained primary schools in
England and Wales at 31st March 1969*

Age	London E.P.A. %	Birmingham E.P.A. %	West Riding E.P.A. %	London, Birmingham and West Riding total %	All England and Wales* %
Under 25 years	32	27	10	26	18
25–34 years	21	40	19	26	22
35–44 years	18	13	26	18	23
45 years and over	28	20	46	30	36
No information	1	0	0	0	0
Total %	100	100	100	100	100
(N)	(145)	(70)	(59)	(274)	(153,259)

* Source *Statistics of Education 1969*, Vol. 4, Table 26. Includes nursery schools and all-age
schools.

The differences between the West Riding project area and the others
have been discussed at some length in the first volume of this series.[1] While the
London, Birmingham and Liverpool project areas were inner districts
suffering a complex of problems of dereliction, population mobility and
housing pressure, the West Riding E.P.A. comprised two small, economically
declining mining villages with a stable and homogeneous population. The
problem of retaining teachers in inner city schools is very great, especially
when alternative posts are available in the suburbs, while in the mining
villages there was not as much alternative employment for any teacher who
may have wished to leave. In fact Table B.7 shows that 34 per cent and
27 per cent in the London and Birmingham project schools respectively
were in their first or second year of teaching, compared with 15 per cent
in the West Riding, and that only 35 per cent and 36 per cent respectively

Table B.7

*Number of years which E.P.A. teachers have spent in the teaching
profession, by project area*

Number of years	London E.P.A. %	Birmingham E.P.A. %	West Riding E.P.A. %	London, Birmingham and West Riding total %
1–2 years	34	27	15	28
3–9 years	29	38	24	30
10 years or more	35	36	61	40
No information	1	0	0	1
Total %	100	100	100	100
(N)	(145)	(70)	(59)	(274)

[1] Chapter 5.

had been in the profession for ten years or more, as against 61 per cent of teachers in the West Riding. Table B.8 further shows that 42 per cent of teachers in London and 36 per cent in Birmingham had been teaching in the same school for less than two years, and only a quarter had stayed for five years or more: in contrast, a half of the West Riding teachers had stayed for this length of time, and indeed over a third had stayed for ten years or longer.

The figures therefore suggest that the inner city schools are staffed to a large extent by young teachers in their first job since leaving college—39 per cent of teachers in London E.P.A. and 36 per cent in Birmingham had held no previous teaching appointment, compared with 20 per cent in the West Riding. The departure of these teachers to take up more attractive posts elsewhere, or to get married or have a baby, creates a constant problem of staff turnover.

Table B.8

Number of years for which teachers have taught in the same school, by project area

Number of years	London E.P.A. %	Birmingham E.P.A. %	West Riding E.P.A. %	London, Birmingham and West Riding total %
Less than 2 years	42	36	29	38
2–4 years	32	37	19	31
5 years or more	24	25	50	29
No information	2	3	3	3
Total %	100	100	100	100
(N)	(145)	(70)	(59)	(274)

Table B.9 is perhaps surprising in that it shows that the London and Birmingham E.P.A. schools had a substantially higher proportion of graduate teachers than the average for all maintained primary schools in England and Wales—in the West Riding E.P.A. schools the proportion was about the same. Nationally there are slightly more graduates among younger than among older teachers, and of course the age of teachers in the London and Birmingham project schools was well below the national average; however the difference in the proportions of graduates in the project schools and schools nationally was not simply due to this, as it was as great for teachers aged 35 or more as it was for teachers below 35. The difference in favour of the E.P.A. schools was also preserved when we took men and women separately: 14·3 per cent of men teachers in the E.P.A. schools were graduates compared with 7·5 per cent of men teachers in all primary schools, and 7·4 per cent of the women E.P.A. teachers were graduates compared with 3·5 per cent nationally. In London there were special reasons for this: the project schools were situated close to a college of education which ran in-service degree courses, and one catholic school there had recruited several teachers from a seminary which gave degrees. We could however find no particularly convincing explanation for the high proportion of graduates in Birmingham, unless it be simply that large cities attract graduates, and in view of the small numbers involved this may have been a chance fluctuation in the particular year the survey took place.

Table B.9

Graduate and non-graduate teachers (including unqualified) by project area, compared with all qualified teachers in maintained primary schools in England and Wales at 31st March 1969

	London E.P.A. %	Birmingham E.P.A. %	West Riding E.P.A. %	London, Birmingham and West Riding total %	All England and Wales* %
Graduates	11	10	3	9	4
Non-graduates	85	85	97	88	96
No information and not classifiable	4	4	0	3	0
Total %	100	100	100	100	100
(N)	(145)	(70)	(59)	(274)	(153,259)

* Source: *Statistics of Education 1969*, Vol. 4, Table 26. Includes nursery schools and all-age schools.

Table B.10 shows a further interesting difference between the London and Birmingham project schools on the one hand and the West Riding schools on the other. While two-thirds of teachers in the former said they were the children of non-manual workers, only two-fifths of teachers in the latter came from a non-manual background. Furthermore, the majority of fathers of the West Riding teachers who were in non-manual occupations had clerical or supervisory jobs, while in the Birmingham and more especially in the London project schools professional or administrative and managerial

Table B.10

Teachers' classifications of their fathers' occupations, by project area

Classification of father's occupation	London E.P.A. %	Birmingham E.P.A. %	West Riding E.P.A. %	London, Birmingham and West Riding total %
Professional or administrative	24	17	7	18
Managerial or executive	26	19	12	21
Clerical or supervisory	17	29	22	21
All non-manual (%)	*67*	*65*	*41*	*60*
Skilled manual	20	23	31	23
Semi-skilled manual	7	7	20	10
Unskilled manual	1	3	8	3
All manual (%)	*28*	*33*	*59*	*36*
No information or not classifiable	6	3	0	4
Total %	100	100	100	100
(N)	(145)	(70)	(59)	(274)

or executive jobs were predominant. The West Riding mining towns have a very homogeneous class structure and the working class backgrounds of the teachers may be no more than a reflection of this, for the towns are geographically fairly isolated. While the London and Birmingham project areas were also overwhelmingly working class, the two cities offer more to teachers from middle class backgrounds than the mining towns can in the way of amenities and attractive places to live. There may however be an additional explanation. It has already been shown that the West Riding teachers were much older and more experienced than the teachers in the inner city schools. It may be the case that teachers from middle class backgrounds tend to take jobs in E.P.A. schools only at the beginning of their career, when they are unable to obtain posts elsewhere, and move out to the more attractive suburban schools when the opportunity arises. Perhaps teachers who themselves have working class origins are more prepared to commit themselves to a lifetime of teaching in an E.P.A. school, though this is only speculation.

If there was less social distance between the West Riding teachers and their pupils, there was also less geographical distance between where they and their pupils lived. Tables B.11 and B.12 show that nearly a quarter of them lived less than half a mile from the school and a half could be at the school within a quarter of an hour. In contrast the Birmingham, and again more especially the London E.P.A. teachers tended to live further away and to have considerably longer travelling times. These differences are undoubtedly related to the availability of accommodation in the three areas, but the result may be that the West Riding teachers have a greater understanding of the home circumstances of the children in their care.

Table B.11

Distance of teacher's home from school, by project area

Distance	London E.P.A. %	Birmingham E.P.A. %	West Riding E.P.A. %	London, Birmingham and West Riding total %
Less than ½ mile	5	7	22	9
Up to 2 miles	16	31	20	21
Up to 5 miles	50	43	34	45
More than 5 miles	26	19	22	23
No information	3	0	2	2
Total %	100	100	100	100
(N)	(145)	(70)	(59)	(274)

Construction and scoring of the attitude scales

The questionnaire asked teachers to complete seven attitude scales, as follows:

Scale A: Community (13 items). Those with high scores believed that the school should play an active role in the local community.

Scale B: Parents (13 items). A high score indicated that the teacher felt that efforts should be made to increase communication between the school and parents.

Scale C: Disadvantaged Children (13 items). Those with high scores held the view that special compensatory education programmes should be set up to help disadvantaged children.

Scale D: Permissiveness (5 items). A high score indicated permissiveness in · views about children's behaviour and self-expression.

Table B.12

Length of teacher's journey from home to school, by project area

Length of journey	London E.P.A. %	Birmingham E.P.A. %	West Riding E.P.A. %	London, Birmingham and West Riding total %
Less than ¼ hour	10	29	49	23
Up to ½ hour	34	40	25	34
Up to ¾ hour	28	24	15	24
More than ¾ hour	25	7	10	17
No information	3	0	0	2
Total %	100	100	100	100
(N)	(145)	(70)	(59)	(274)

Scale E: Physical Punishment (6 items). Those with high scores disapproved of the use of physical punishment in schools.

Scale F: Noise (5 items). A high score showed tolerance of noise in the classroom.

Scale G: Less Able Children (6 items). Those with high scores felt that teaching less able children was interesting and worthwhile.

Scales D, E, F and G were devised by C. J. Tuppen[1] and used in the study of streaming in primary schools conducted by the National Foundation for Educational Research.[2] Items in the scales were derived from un-structured interviews with 31 junior school teachers. The first versions were piloted on further samples of teachers, and Guttman scales were constructed on the basis of their responses. Scales D, E and F reached acceptable levels of reproducibility, but scale G failed to reach the criterion level and is therefore treated as a factor scale whose internal consistency, using Cronbach's alpha coefficient, is ·70.

Scales A, B and C were constructed by Dr. Terence Lee[3] especially for the E.P.A. survey. Eighty-one statements suggested by student teachers were included in a pilot questionnaire which also contained the Tuppen scales. This questionnaire was completed by a quota sample of 150 primary school teachers in non-E.P.A. schools in six areas of England and Wales, the sample being designed in such a way as to be representative in age, sex and type of school (infant, junior, or junior with infants) of all teachers in

---

[1] For details of the scales see *Manual for the use of Teacher's Attitude Scales (Streaming)*, National Foundation for Educational Research, November 1967.

[2] Joan C. Barker Lunn, *Streaming in the Primary School*, National Foundation for Educational Research, 1970.

[3] See above, p. 24.

maintained primary schools. The results were analysed by the method of Guttman scalogram analysis, and the original 81 items were reduced to 39, 13 per scale. Scales B and C both satisfied the Guttman criterion of ·9 reproducibility, but scale A only reached ·85 and should therefore be interpreted with a little caution.

In the questionnaire distributed to teachers items from the different scales were presented in randomised order, and respondents did not know the scale to which an item belonged. In the copy of the questionnaire in the Appendix to this section we have indicated against each item the scale to which it belongs and the way in which it is scored, but of course this information did not appear in the original version. It will be noticed that while agreement with some items scores one, agreement with others scores zero. These "negative" or "reversed" items are included in order to off-set "response set": the tendency of some respondents to answer all items in the same way. The number of positive and negative items in each scale is given below:

	Positive	*Negative*
Scale A	9	4
Scale B	4	9
Scale C	8	5
Scale D	2	3
Scale E	2	4
Scale F	2	3
Scale G	5	1

The numbers are unequal because of the elimination of items from the pilot versions of the scales by scalogram analysis.

The notion of reproducibility in Guttman scaling is based on the idea that the items comprising a scale can be rank-ordered in terms of their "difficulty". "Difficulty" is defined by the number of people who give the "scored" response to an item, that is, the response which indicates that they possess the quality measured by the scale. The item to which the fewest respondents give the scored response is regarded as the most "difficult", and *vice versa*. If we postulate a certain order of difficulty among the items we should be able to infer from the respondent's total score on a Guttman scale the individual items to which he gave the scored response. For example, if a respondent gains a total score of four on a scale consisting of five items we would infer that he gave the scored response to all items except the most "difficult" one. "Reproducibility" is measured by the similarity in a sample of respondents between the inferred and the actual distribution of scored responses. In order to maximise reproducibility the cut-off point between .the scored and the non-scored response to an item can be varied. Thus, for instance, if items have five possible responses ranging from "strongly agree" to "strongly disagree" the cut-off point for one item in a scale may be taken after "strongly agree", for another after "agree", and for yet another after the middle point, "neutral".

Although we did not submit the responses of the E.P.A. teachers to scalogram analysis, we were able to compare the order of difficulty of items in the E.P.A. sample with that found in the construction samples. Details of this comparison are given in Table B.13, which is based on figures including teachers in Liverpool E.P.A.

Table B.13
Guttman attitude scales: comparison of the order of difficulty of items found in the E.P.A. sample with that obtained in the construction samples*

Item	% of respondents giving the scored response		Order of difficulty of items	
	Construction sample	E.P.A. sample	Construction sample	E.P.A. sample
Scale A: Community				
School children should pay fairly frequent visits to local firms and places of interest.	91	98	1	1
Teachers should use their special knowledge to help social workers in the community.	84	94	2	2
At least one way in which country schools excel over town schools is that they are more a part of the community.	81	85	3	4
Schools are for teaching children academic subjects; there is too strong a tendency nowadays to turn them into social centres.	75	84	4	5
I have better things to do with my time than helping to solve local problems.	72	90	5 ⎫	3
Local "leading citizens" should not be encouraged to offer their opinions on the affairs of a school.	72	65	5 ⎭	10
Teachers should accept positions of leadership in the community.	63	79	7	6
Every school should have close relations with the local newspaper.	60	75	8	7
Teachers should be willing to visit problem families occasionally out of school hours.	58	72	9	9
Teachers have no special obligation in the community apart from doing their job in the school.	47	73	10	8
The morale of a school depends as much on the neighbourhood from which it draws its children as on the headmaster and teachers.	43	57	11	11
It is good for a school if both the teachers and the children live in the local area.	38	48	12	12
Schoolteachers are naturally the leaders of any community.	14	37	13	13
Scale B: Parents				
I always find it helpful and enlightening to have a talk with parents and only the occasional one is difficult.	92	96	1	2

* Based on figures including teachers in Liverpool E.P.A.

Table B.13 continued

Item	% of respondents giving the scored response		Order of difficulty of items	
	Construction sample	E.P.A. sample	Construction sample	E.P.A. sample
Most parents are pretty reasonable about their children's school problems.	90	94	2	6
If I am teaching in a school which has a parent-teacher association I do my best to avoid the meetings.	88	96	3 ⎫	2
Every school should have an open day to discuss their objectives with the parents.	88	97	3 ⎪	1
If the parents want to know anything about the children in my class I prefer them to discuss it with the headmaster and not with me.	88	95	3 ⎭	4
Many parents couldn't care less about their child's school life and it is not part of the teacher's job to persuade them to care.	82	91	6	7
A report once each term is sufficient communication between teachers and parents.	80	88	7	8
Parents should continually be encouraged to discuss their children's progress with teachers.	79	95	8	4
Many parents try to meddle too much in their child's education.	65	86	9	9
It should be made clear that parents have no say in any punishment which their child receives at school, provided that it is legal.	45	59	10	10
I don't want parents telling me what to do with their child at school.	29	42	11	11
Most parents exaggerate the abilities and virtues of their own children.	28	39	12	12
Marginal of construction sample unknown:				
Teachers and parents are responsible for quite different aspects of the child and they should not interfere with each other.		90		
Scale C: Disadvantaged Children				
Special help for educationally deprived children is money down the drain.	95	98	1 ⎫	1 ⎫
Children from poor homes should receive special encouragement and help from their teachers.	95	98	1 ⎭	1 ⎪
Everything possible should be done educationally to compensate children from poor homes.	94	98	3	1 ⎭

Table B.13 continued

Item	% of respondents giving the scored response		Order of difficulty of items	
	Construction sample	E.P.A. sample	Construction sample	E.P.A. sample
It is wasteful to spend extra money and energy on children who are unlikely to do anything but unskilled manual labour.	93	97	4	4
Disadvantaged children come from poor degenerate stock, there is nothing much you can do about it educationally.	93	94	4	5
Deprived children should be taught by teachers specially chosen for their interest and sympathy.	89	94	6	5
There is too much talk about underprivileged children and not enough about the taxpayer.	89	87	6	11
Children from poor homes should be given special opportunities to take part in after-school activities.	85	94	8	5
Extra provision of staff and equipment should be made so that children in poor areas can have after-school activities.	83	92	9	10
Deprived children should be taught in smaller classes than others even though this may raise the cost of education.	83	94	9	5
It is not fair to other children to spend money on areas designated as educationally deprived.	83	94	9	5
Children from the worst areas should be given the best schools to make up for their backgrounds.	48	68	12	12
Disadvantaged children should be given a free holiday every year at the ratepayer's expense.	43	65	13	13
Scale D: Permissiveness				
I cannot stand children fidgeting in class.	90	94	1	1
Teachers should demand clean hands in school.	73	86	2	2
Children must be taught to have decent manners.	56	81	3	3
Naturalness is more important than good manners.	27	47	4	4
Opportunities for self-expression through movement, painting and writing poetry are more important than concentrating on the "3 Rs".	13	26	5	5

Table B.13 continued

Item	% of respondents giving the scored response		Order of difficulty of items	
	Construction sample	E.P.A. sample	Construction sample	E.P.A. sample
Scale E: Physical Punishment				
Physical punishment is out of the question and completely unnecessary.	83	83	1	1
I'm quite prepared to spank bottoms for disobeying rules.	53	61	2	2
An occasional hard slap does children no harm.	31	33	3	3
Physical punishment does no good at all to any child.	25	28	4	4
I think a good slap in the right place at the right time does an awful lot of good.	19	12	5	5
If children in my class are insolent they have to be slapped.	9	12	6	5
Scale F: Noise in the classroom				
I would not allow talking in a class of 35 or more children.	84	93	1	1
I don't mind a reasonably high working noise in my class.	75	82	2	2
A quiet atmosphere is the one best suited for all school work.	53	66	3	3
There is too much emphasis on cutting down noise in schools.	30	24	4	5
Nothing worthwhile will be achieved by a class that talks while it works.	20	25	5	4

Whilst the order of difficulty of items in the Tuppen scales (D, E and F) was almost perfectly preserved in the E.P.A. sample, there was some discrepancy between the E.P.A. sample and the construction sample in the case of the specially designed scales A, B and C. This is partly because there are more items on these scales and therefore more possible ways of ordering the items, and also because the percentages of respondents giving the scored response to each item are less evenly spaced in scales A, B and C than in scales D, E and F. The discrepancy gives further reason for interpreting the results of scales A, B and C cautiously.

Because they were specially constructed for the E.P.A. Project there is no proper comparative data available for the scales Community, Parents and Disadvantaged Children. It would be unwise to base too much on a comparison with the construction sample, for although it was intended to be representative in age, sex and type of school of all teachers in maintained primary schools in England and Wales, nevertheless it was only a small quota sample. We have no guarantee that a larger and properly random sample of teachers would not yield a different pattern of responses.

Nevertheless the consistency of the differences between the E.P.A. and the construction sample is remarkable. Of the 38 items on the three scales which were compared in Table B.13, a higher proportion of the E.P.A. sample gave the scored response to all but two. Thus their replies suggested that they were more likely than teachers nationally to think that the school should play an active role in the community, that teachers should make efforts to increase contacts with parents, and that special compensatory programmes should be set up to help disadvantaged children. These three points were major goals of the E.P.A. Project, and when the survey of teachers was conducted the project teams had already been in contact with schools for several months. It is therefore not possible to say whether teachers in disadvantaged schools generally would share these attitudes, or whether the attitudes developed as a result of the project teams' presence. In either case, the attitudes must have helped the success of the E.P.A. programmes.

We have no details of the construction sample for scales D, E and F, and so we cannot draw any conclusions from the E.P.A. teachers' greater apparent permissiveness, disapproval of physical punishment and tolerance of noise in the classroom over the teachers in the construction sample. However nationally comparable results are available for these scales from the National Foundation for Educational Research's study of streaming,[1] and these are discussed below.[2]

In scoring the attitude scales people with more than two missing items on scales A, B and C and more than one on scales D, E, F and G were omitted from the analysis. This resulted in the loss of the following numbers from the total of 302 respondents in all four project areas, including Liverpool:

Scale	Number of respondents lost
A	6
B	9
C	7
D	10
E	9
F	5
G	7

Where incomplete scales were retained, total score was calculated on the assumption that the best estimate of a respondent's score on a missing item was his mean score on the remaining items in the scale.

Relationship between attitudes and biographical data

When the teacher questionnaire was designed no detailed hypotheses were formulated concerning the relationship between teachers' attitudes and their personal characteristics and career histories, and indeed perhaps not enough was known about teachers' attitudes to allow the formulation of hypotheses specific to E.P.A. teachers. Thus in the analysis of the data exploratory rather than hypothesis testing techniques had to be used. A cross-tabulation was made between high and low scores on each of the attitude scales (taking the dividing point as that which gave the most even split among respondents) and each one of the following biographical variables: sex, age, number of

---

[1] C. Barker-Lunn, *op. cit.*

[2] Page 42 ff.

years in the teaching profession, number of years in the teacher's present school, type of school, type of post, qualification, whether the teacher had ever held a job for more than six months outside the teaching profession, and length of journey from home to school. χ^2 was calculated for each cross-tabulation, and although it had no meaning in this context as a test of significance (for the teachers surveyed did not form a random sample of a larger population), the associated probability value was used as a convenient criterion of the importance of the relationship between the attitude scale score and the biographical variable. Table B.14 lists all the relationships which were found where χ^2 had a probability smaller than ·05, and indicates whether the relationship was positive or inverse with the biographical variable as classified. For example, it shows that women were more likely than men to be interested in teaching less able children, and that teachers aged less than 35 years were more favourable to community participation than those aged 35 or more.

Some of the relationships reported in Table B.14 are not of any real interest, but are merely chance by-products of other associations in the data. There is, for instance, an apparent relationship between tolerance of noise in the classroom and length of journey to work, but this strange finding is probably a result of the fact firstly that younger teachers tended to be more tolerant of noise, secondly that there were more young teachers in London and Birmingham than in the West Riding, and thirdly that teachers in London and Birmingham generally had a longer journey to work. Other relationships emerged for which we could find no obvious explanation and which may represent a purely coincidental association in this particular group of teachers, such as that between length of journey to school and favourability to compensatory programmes for disadvantaged children, or between type of post and interest in teaching less able children.

Relationships between personal characteristics of teachers and their attitudes which are of more substantive interest are set out in detail in Table B.15. The cross-tabulations include teachers in the Liverpool project schools who took part in the survey and exclude those for whom there was missing information on either of the two variables: hence the total number of teachers on which each cross-tabulation is based is variable.

We found that the younger teachers were more likely than teachers aged 35 or more to favour the school's playing an active role in the community. Age is highly correlated with length of service, and not surprisingly it also emerged that those who had been in the teaching profession for less than seven years were more oriented towards the community than teachers of longer standing, as also were those who had taught in their present school for less than two and a half years when compared with those who had given more years service. These relationships are doubtless a product of changes in teaching philosophy which mean that schools tend to be much more outward looking than they were in the past. However, it is interesting to note that the correlation between community attitudes and length of service in present school was preserved even when we controlled for the age of the teacher: if a teacher aged 35 or more had taught in the project school for less than two and a half years, he also was likely to think the school should play an active role in the community. It seems that an accumulation of experience in E.P.A. schools affects attitudes independently of age.

Interestingly, there was no relationship at all between age or experience and attitudes towards contacts with parents; teachers of all types seemed

Table B.14

Relationships between attitude scale scores and biographical variables*

Note: Relationships are indicated only where χ^2 has a probability smaller than ·05.

"+" indicates a positive relationship.

"−" indicates an inverse relationship.

	Attitude Scale						
	A favourability to community participation	B favourability to contacts with parents	C favourability to compensatory programmes for disadvantaged children	D permissiveness	E disapproval of physical punishment	F tolerance of noise in the classroom	G interest in teaching less able children
Sex 0: male 1: female							+
Age 0: less than 35 years 1: 35 years or more	−				−		
Years in teaching 0: less than 7 years 1: 7 years or more		−			−		
Years in present school 0: less than 2½ years 1: 2½ years or more					−		
Type of school 0: infant 1: junior with infants 2: junior				−	−		−
Type of post 0: assistant teacher 1: graded post or head							+
Qualification 0: non-graduate 1: graduate					+		
Jobs outside teaching 0: no job outside teaching 1: work experience outside teaching	+				+		
Journey to school 0: up to ½ hour 1: ½ hour or more			+			+	

* Based on figures including teachers in Liverpool E.P.A.

to agree in thinking this to be important. Contact with parents can however have very different ends: at one extreme it can mean giving the parent the information he needs to help the school do what it sees as best, while at the other it can mean consulting the parent as someone with a good deal

Table B.15

*Relationships between attitude scale scores and
various characteristics of teachers**

	High scorers %	Low scorers %	All %	All (N)
Scale A : Community				
(i) age less than 35 years	68	32	100	(149)
age 35 years or more	55	45	100	(138)
(ii) teaching for less than 7 years	69	31	100	(140)
teaching for 7 years or more	56	44	100	(145)
(iii) in present school less than 2½ years	69	31	100	(154)
in present school 2½ years or more	53	47	100	(125)
Scale B : Parents				
(iv) no job outside teaching	35	65	100	(198)
work experience outside teaching	54	46	100	(72)
Scale D : Permissiveness				
(v) teaching for less than 7 years	57	43	100	(143)
teaching for 7 years or more	43	57	100	(145)
(vi) infant school teachers	61	39	100	(82)
junior with infants school teachers	45	55	100	(110)
junior school teachers	46	54	100	(91)
Scale E : Physical Punishment				
(vii) non-graduates	36	64	100	(261)
graduates	68	32	100	(25)
(viii) no job outside teaching	35	65	100	(203)
work experience outside teaching	53	47	100	(73)
Scale F : Noise				
(ix) age less than 35 years	41	59	100	(153)
age 35 years or more	26	74	100	(142)
(x) teaching for less than 7 years	43	57	100	(144)
teaching for 7 years or more	26	74	100	(149)
(xi) infant school teachers	48	52	100	(83)
junior with infants school teachers	24	76	100	(111)
junior school teachers	32	68	100	(94)
Scale G : Less Able Children				
(xii) men teachers	38	62	100	(74)
women teachers	62	38	100	(221)

* Figures include teachers in Liverpool E.P.A.

of knowledge about his child and an important say in how the child should
be treated. Scale B did not tap this dimension but measured belief in the
principle of communication with parents *per se*. It may be that this principle
is now so well established that a focus on the purpose of contacts with
parents would have revealed a greater variation in teachers' attitudes.

We did find, however, that teachers who had work experience outside
teaching were even more likely to favour contacts with parents than their

colleagues. It may be that having seen the teaching profession from outside, perhaps as parents themselves, mature entrants to the profession are less insistent on professional boundaries. This would be consistent with the further finding that such teachers are more likely to disapprove of physical punishment than teachers whose entire work experience has been within the teaching profession.

Favourability to compensatory programmes for disadvantaged children did not seem to relate to any biographical variable except length of journey to school, with which it had an inexplicable inverse correlation. We found however that teachers with shorter teaching experience were more permissive in what they regarded as acceptable behaviour on the part of the child, and more tolerant of noise in the classroom. The younger teachers were also more tolerant of noise than the older, but though it appeared at first that those who had taught in their present school for a short time only were also more tolerant, the relationship vanished when age was controlled.

Permissiveness both of behaviour and of noise has clearly been an important trend in educational thinking in recent years; it is also particularly characteristic of the infant school, and this was confirmed in the responses of the E.P.A. teachers. We were surprised however to find that teachers in junior with infants schools were, if anything, less permissive in these respects than their colleagues in junior schools. Whether this was a result purely of coincidence, or whether it is related to organisational features of junior with infants schools—perhaps their larger size—we can only guess.

Despite the greater permissiveness of the younger and less experienced teachers they were equally as likely as their older colleagues to approve of physical punishment; nor was there any large difference between infant and junior teachers in this respect. It is often said that though students may be encouraged in college not to use physical punishment, this position is quickly abandoned in the real classroom situation. The evidence from the survey suggests that this somewhat cynical view is correct. We did find however that graduate teachers were less likely to favour physical punishment than those without degrees, which may be because graduate teachers come more often from middle class backgrounds.

We found that sex affected scores on only one attitude scale, but that with that scale the relationship was extremely marked. Sixty-two per cent of women had high scores on scale G measuring interest in teaching less able children, compared with only 38 per cent of men. It also appeared that infant school teachers were more interested in less able children, but this factor was inextricable from the much higher proportion of women teachers in infant schools. Women choose much more often than men to teach very young children, and their interest in less able children may well be a further aspect of this. In addition, the most prestigious positions in schools are generally in charge of the oldest and cleverest children, and it is not implausible that the lack of interest shown by men in less able children is due to their greater ambitiousness.

Comparison of the attitudes of E.P.A. teachers with a national sample

In the study of streaming carried out by the National Foundation for Educational Research, scales D, E, F and G were used to compare the attitudes of teachers in 36 matched pairs of streamed and unstreamed junior schools.[1] Because of the requirements of the matching process and

---

[1] J. C. Barker-Lunn, *op. cit.*

because each school in the study had to have at least a two form entry, the schools could not be said to be a representative sample of all junior schools in England and Wales. The schools in the N.F.E.R. study were generally bigger than the E.P.A. schools and only a very small proportion had infant departments, but like the E.P.A. schools they were almost all urban. The distribution of occupations among the fathers of pupils in the N.F.E.R. sample was much more similar to the national distribution than in the E.P.A. schools, which were of course overwhelmingly working class, and in this sense the N.F.E.R. sample can be said to provide a non-E.P.A. comparison.

As the N.F.E.R. study had been concerned with junior school teachers only we divided the E.P.A. teachers into two groups of junior and infant school teachers for comparison. The way the survey had been administered in the London and West Riding E.P.A.s had made it possible to distinguish infant and junior teachers in junior with infants schools, but unfortunately this could not be done in Birmingham, and teachers in junior with infants schools there were omitted. Liverpool teachers were excluded altogether because of their low response rate. It was not possible to break down the E.P.A. schools further into streamed and unstreamed groups, as numbers would have been very small once single form entry schools had been excluded.

The detailed comparisons between the E.P.A. and the N.F.E.R. schools are shown in Figures B(1) to B(8). On each of the four attitude scales the frequency distribution of the scores of E.P.A. junior teachers is compared first with the distribution of scores in streamed and unstreamed junior schools in the N.F.E.R. sample, and second with the scores of E.P.A. infant teachers. For each comparison a rank order correlation coefficient, Kendall's Tau_b, has been calculated between attitude scale score and a dummy binary variable giving the group to which the teacher belongs. Thus if Tau_b is large, there is an important difference between the scores of the E.P.A. junior teachers and the group with which they are compared. Neither the N.F.E.R. nor the E.P.A. teachers were random samples from larger populations, and so the concepts of significance testing do not apply. However, for each comparison we also report the probability (using a two-tailed test) of getting the calculated value of Tau_b if these were random samples and there were no association between group and attitude score in the population sampled. These probability levels are not intended as significance tests, but simply give a convenient indication of the importance of the correlation, for the size of Tau_b depends not only on the degree of correlation between the variables, but also on the number of values each has.

The N.F.E.R. study of streaming had found that there was a general trend towards permissiveness between 1964 and 1966, but that at the later date teachers in unstreamed schools were still slightly more permissive than those in streamed schools. Figure B(1) shows that the E.P.A. junior teachers surveyed in 1968 were considerably more permissive than either group, a finding which may reflect a continuing trend towards permissiveness. The generally shorter teaching experience of the E.P.A. teachers may also be a factor here, as we have already shown that teachers with less experience are more likely to be permissive.[1] However the necessity of excluding from the comparison a large number of teachers in junior with infants schools in

---

[1] Table B.15.

Figure B(1): Permissiveness: E.P.A. junior teachers compared with national samples of teachers
in streamed and unstreamed junior schools

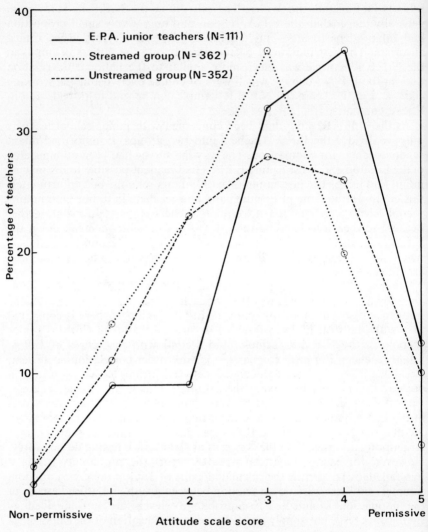

E.P.A. junior teachers with streamed group: Tau$_b$ = ·19; P< ·01

E.P.A. junior teachers with unstreamed group: Tau$_b$ = ·10; P< ·01

Birmingham gives more weight to the older West Riding teachers and redresses the age balance somewhat.

As the teaching practices in infant schools would lead us to expect, E.P.A. infant teachers were yet more permissive than their colleagues in the junior school. Figure B(2) shows however that the scores of these two groups were closer together than the scores of the E.P.A. junior teachers were to those of the N.F.E.R. samples.

It appears from Figure B(3) that junior teachers were also less likely to approve of physical punishment than teachers in the N.F.E.R. sample, though the difference was not as great as on the permissiveness scale. The factors which explained the greater permissiveness of the E.P.A. teachers do not apply here, as the N.F.E.R. found no consistent change in attitudes towards physical punishment between 1964 and 1966, and disapproval of physical punishment did not appear to correlate with age. The greater reluctance of the E.P.A. teachers to use physical punishment is therefore surprising, as one would expect them generally to face greater problems of discipline. It must be stressed, however, that the difference between the E.P.A. teachers and the rest is small, and that the majority of both still advocated its use. We see in Figure B(4) that the E.P.A. infant teachers were only slightly less in favour of physical punishment than the junior teachers, but there was a slight tendency in that direction which the less sensitive χ^2 test reported in Table B.14 had failed to pick up.

Figure B(2): Permissiveness: E.P.A. junior teachers compared with E.P.A. infant teachers

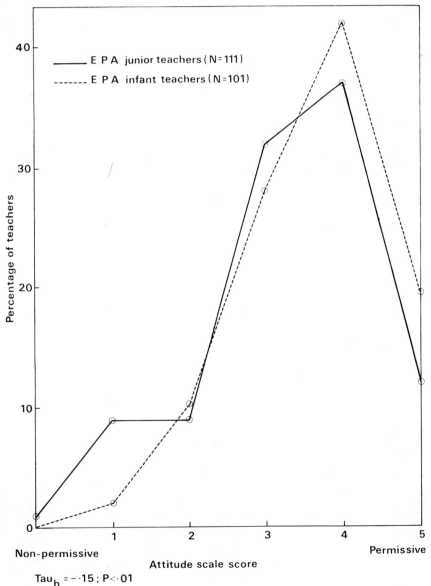

Percentage of teachers

——— E P A junior teachers (N = 111)

------- E P A infant teachers (N = 101)

Non-permissive

Permissive

Attitude scale score

$\text{Tau}_b = -\cdot15 ; P < \cdot01$

Figure B(3): Attitudes to physical punishment: E.P.A. junior teachers compared with national samples of teachers in streamed and unstreamed junior schools

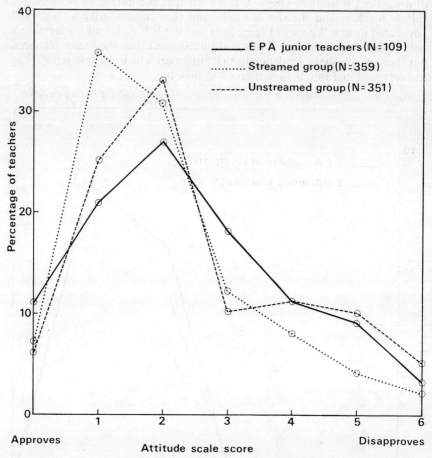

E.P.A. junior teachers with streamed group: Tau_b= ·08; P< ·025

E.P.A. junior teachers with unstreamed group: Tau_b= ·03; P> ·05

Figure B(4) : Attitudes to physical punishment : E.P.A. junior teachers compared with E.P.A. infant teachers

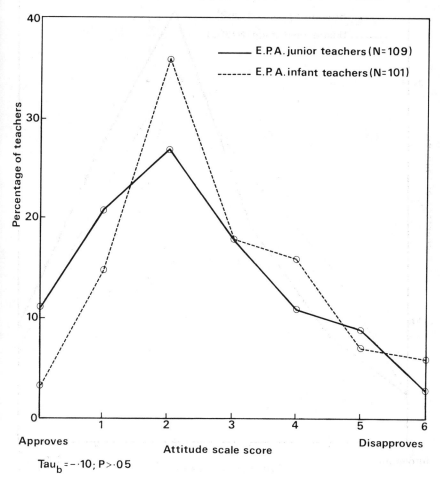

Figure B(5): Attitudes to noise in the classroom: E.P.A. junior teachers compared with national samples of teachers in streamed and unstreamed junior schools

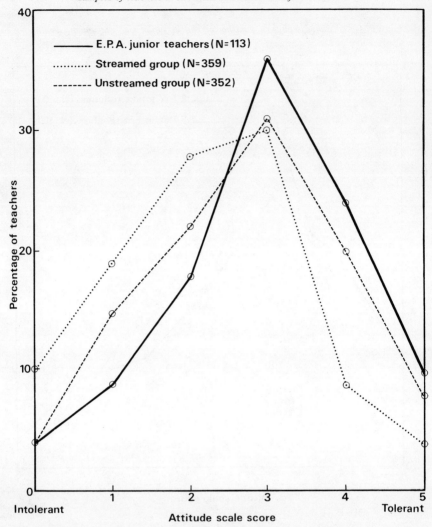

E.P.A. junior teachers with streamed group : Tau$_b$ = · 23 ; P< · 01
E.P.A. junior teachers with unstreamed group : Tau$_b$ = · 07 ; P> · 05

Attitudes towards noise in the classroom are again related to age and experience, and so the greater tolerance which Figure B(5) shows the E.P.A. teachers to have could have been predicted from their relative youth. Figure B(6) re-asserts what has already been established in Table B.15, that the E.P.A. infant teachers were more tolerant of noise than the junior teachers.

In Figure B(7) we see a reverse of the previous pattern, with E.P.A. teachers appearing less interested in less able children than their non-E.P.A. counterparts. There is also very little difference between E.P.A. infant and junior school teachers on this scale (Figure B(8)). This finding was quite unexpected, as the N.F.E.R. study found a positive association between this dimension and the other three. It also has serious implications, for Section A has amply demonstrated the extent of the problem of low achievement in the project schools. It may be that the attitudes of E.P.A. teachers are based on a more realistic assessment of the problems of teaching less able children than could be made by teachers in schools where very few children are backward, or the sheer numbers of less able children in the E.P.A. schools may cause additional difficulties. Alternatively, the E.P.A. teacher's conception of a less able child may be of someone with much more serious learning problems than a non-E.P.A. teacher would imagine.

We can say, then, that E.P.A. teachers appear to be more permissive, more tolerant of noise and less approving of physical punishment than teachers in non-E.P.A. schools, though it is unclear to what extent the first two features represent an adaptation to the conditions in E.P.A. schools, and to what extent they are a product of the age structure of the staff.

Figure B(6): Attitudes to noise in the classroom: E.P.A. junior teachers compared with E.P.A. infant teachers

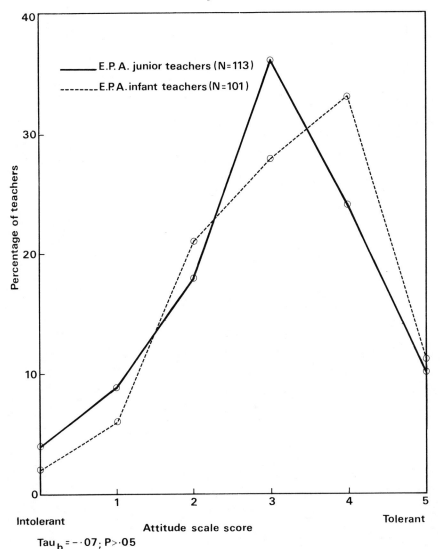

E.P.A. junior teachers (N=113)

E.P.A. infant teachers (N=101)

Percentage of teachers

Intolerant

Attitude scale score

Tolerant

$Tau_b = -\cdot 07; P > \cdot 05$

Figure B(7): Attitudes to less able children: E.P.A. junior teachers compared with national samples of teachers in streamed and unstreamed junior schools

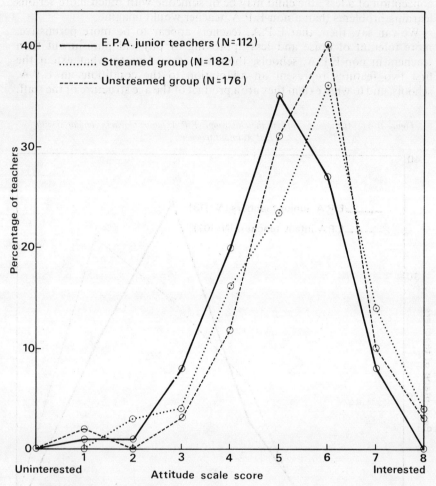

E.P.A. teachers with streamed group: Tau$_b$ = −·14; P< ·01

E.P.A. teachers with unstreamed group: Tau$_b$ = −·16; P< ·01

Figure B(8) : Attitudes to less able children: E.P.A. junior teachers compared with E.P.A. infant teachers

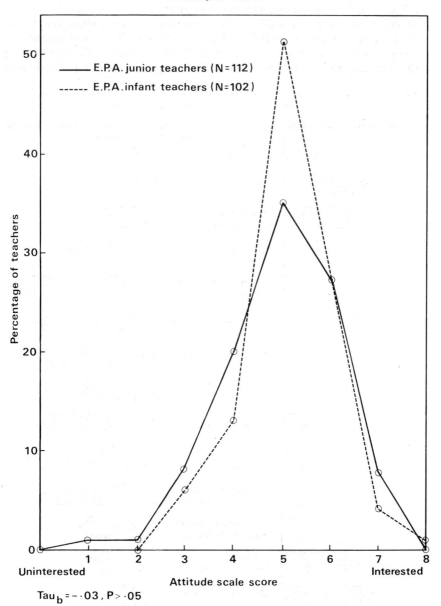

Tau$_b$ = – ·03 , P> ·05

On the other hand, they are less interested in teaching less able children, and whatever the explanation for this, it must affect their satisfaction with their teaching position.

Job satisfaction of E.P.A. teachers

Job satisfaction was assessed by two sets of questions which were originally designed for use in the study of probationary teachers carried out by the Institute of Education at Bristol University.[1] The first asked teachers to compare various aspects of their job with the jobs of friends of approximately the same age and with equivalent qualifications; the second asked them to

Figure B(9): E.P.A. teachers' comparisons of their jobs with jobs of friends of approximately the same age and with equivalent qualifications

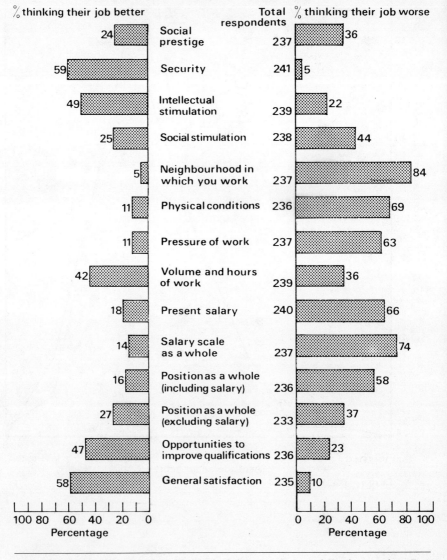

% thinking their job better		Total respondents	% thinking their job worse
24	Social prestige	237	36
59	Security	241	5
49	Intellectual stimulation	239	22
25	Social stimulation	238	44
5	Neighbourhood in which you work	237	84
11	Physical conditions	236	69
11	Pressure of work	237	63
42	Volume and hours of work	239	36
18	Present salary	240	66
14	Salary scale as a whole	237	74
16	Position as a whole (including salary)	236	58
27	Position as a whole (excluding salary)	233	37
47	Opportunities to improve qualifications	236	23
58	General satisfaction	235	10

100 80   60   40   20   0   0   20   40   60   80 100
Percentage   Percentage

[1] J. K. Taylor and I. R. Dale, with M. A. Brimer, *A Survey of Teachers in their First Year of Service,* University of Bristol, 1971.

Figure B(10): E.P.A. teachers' comparisons of their teaching situation with that of teachers they know in other schools

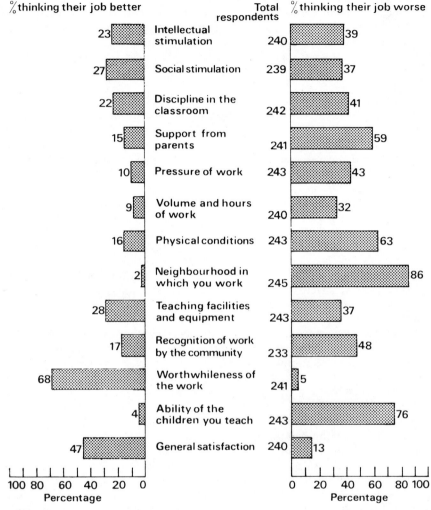

% thinking their job better   Total   % thinking their job worse
                                        respondents

% thinking their job better		Total respondents	% thinking their job worse
23	Intellectual stimulation	240	39
27	Social stimulation	239	37
22	Discipline in the classroom	242	41
15	Support from parents	241	59
10	Pressure of work	243	43
9	Volume and hours of work	240	32
16	Physical conditions	243	63
2	Neighbourhood in which you work	245	86
28	Teaching facilities and equipment	243	37
17	Recognition of work by the community	233	48
68	Worthwhileness of the work	241	5
4	Ability of the children you teach	243	76
47	General satisfaction	240	13

100 80 60 40 20 0
Percentage

0 20 40 60 80 100
Percentage

compare various aspects of their teaching situation with that of teachers they knew in other schools. Some aspects were common to both sets of comparisons while others were relevant only to one, and for each the teacher had a choice of seven responses ranging from "very much better" to "very much worse". Each comparison was treated as meaningful in its own right and responses were not summed to form any kind of scale.

Responses to the two sets of comparisons are shown in Figures B(9) and B(10). Those giving the answers "very much better", "a good deal better", or "slightly better" have been grouped together, and similarly with those thinking their job worse. Those who thought their job was "about the same" are not shown, and hence percentages do not total to 100. As elsewhere, teachers in Liverpool E.P.A. are excluded.

Some teachers felt they could not make comparative judgments about some aspects of their job, and the graphs also show the numbers on which the percentages are based, out of a possible total of 274 respondents.

Non-response in the comparisons with friends ranged from 12 per cent to 15 per cent, while in the comparisons with teachers in other schools non-response was slightly lower, generally between 11 per cent and 13 per cent. The difference was largely due to the West Riding teachers who found it very difficult to make comparisons with friends with equivalent qualifications, because the range of jobs available to such people in the two mining towns was very limited.[1] Non-response was lowest in Birmingham, where it ran at only 6 per cent or 7 per cent on both sets of comparisons.

When comparing their jobs with the jobs of friends, more teachers thought they were better off than thought they were worse off in respect of security, intellectual stimulation, volume and hours of work, opportunities to improve qualifications, and general satisfaction, though in only two of these, security and general satisfaction, did a majority of teachers think their job was better. More teachers thought they were worse off than thought they were better off in regard to social prestige, social stimulation, the neighbourhood in which they worked, physical conditions, pressure of work, present salary, salary scale as a whole, and position as a whole including and excluding salary. In six of these aspects more than half of the respondents thought they were worse off than their friends: the aspect of their work which compared least favourably was the neighbourhood, with 84 per cent saying it was worse, but physical conditions, pressure of work and salary levels were also major sources of discontent.

Teachers in the project schools appeared to be in an even worse position when they compared themselves with teachers in other schools. In eleven of the thirteen aspects considered, the number thinking they were worse off was greater than the number thinking they were better off. Intellectual stimulation, social stimulation, discipline, support from parents, pressure of work, volume and hours of work, physical conditions, neighbourhood, teaching facilities and equipment, recognition of work by the community, and the ability of the children were all the object of unfavourable comparisons, and once again neighbourhood and physical conditions compared particularly badly, together this time with support from parents and the ability of the children. On the remaining two items responses were totally reversed, for the E.P.A. teachers tended to feel that both the worthwhileness of their work and the general satisfaction it gave were greater than for teachers elsewhere.

Both sets of comparisons present a picture of a teaching force for which the satisfaction of doing a worthwhile job is balanced against low pay, low status and difficult working conditions. However this satisfaction is evidently not sufficient compensation for many, for we have seen above that teacher turnover in the inner city project schools was extremely high.[2]

Differences in job satisfaction between project areas

Teachers' feelings about the work situation were not the same in the three areas, but varied according to local circumstances. Tables B.16 and B.17 set out the details of responses to the job satisfaction questions in each area. As we had attempted complete coverage of teachers in the project schools it was not appropriate to use significance tests, and instead we

---

[1] Tables B.16 and B.17 give exact figures for non-response in the West Riding project schools.
[2] See page 29.

discuss below those differences between areas which were both consistent[1] and fairly big.

Several dimensions emerged on which areas differed. The first related to the school's place in the community, and included support from parents, neighbourhood, and recognition of work by the community at large. On each of these items teachers in the West Riding schools expressed least dissatisfaction and teachers in Birmingham most, a difference which reflects the type of population served by the project schools in each area. The West Riding mining towns had an extremely stable population, and many parents had attended the same school as their children.[2] In contrast, the project schools in Birmingham were in what sociologists call a "transitional" area: an area in which newcomers to the city tended to settle, which was racially mixed, and which, due both to the influx of immigrants and the demolition of old houses, had an extremely mobile population. These factors were also reflected in teachers' views about their pupils: teachers in the West Riding were less likely than teachers in either of the other areas to complain about discipline problems, and only 63 per cent of them thought that the ability of their pupils was worse than in other schools, compared with 88 per cent in Birmingham. The opinion of the Birmingham teachers was confirmed by the survey of attainment, which showed the performance of pupils in the Birmingham project schools on standardized tests of vocabulary and reading to be far below that of pupils in other areas.[3]

A further dimension on which areas were contrasted concerned the physical conditions of work and teaching facilities and equipment, with teachers in Birmingham again the least satisfied of the three. In the London project schools more teachers felt that facilities and equipment were better than in other schools than felt that they were worse, a finding which reflects the Inner London Education Authority's policy of generosity in these respects.

With regard to salary the London teachers were more discontented than the rest. Both the cost of living and salaries generally are higher in London, and presumably it was felt that the London allowance did not fully compensate for the difference.[4] However in respect of the opportunity to improve qualifications, teachers in both London and Birmingham were quite likely to think their job better than others, though teachers in the West Riding did not agree. The West Riding teachers were, of course, older on average, and so this opportunity was probably less important to them, but they were also more isolated from both colleges of education and universities.

Finally it appeared that when comparing themselves with friends in other jobs teachers in the West Riding were more likely than teachers in London or Birmingham to feel that they had greater pressure of work and greater volume and hours of work. There is no obvious explanation for this unless it be that jobs in big cities are felt to be generally more pressured. However fluctuations in the data must be expected with such small numbers, especially in view of the general difficulty which West Riding teachers had in comparing teaching with other jobs.

---

[1] i.e. when an area has both fewer teachers saying "better" and more saying "worse", or *vice versa*, than the other areas it is being compared with.

[2] This emerged from the survey of parents; see page 83 below.

[3] See Section A.

[4] Recent demands for an increased London allowance confirm this.

Table B.16

Teachers' comparisons of their jobs with the jobs of friends of approximately the same age and with equivalent qualifications, by project area

	% giving response			Total %	Total no. respondents	No. non-respondents
	better	same	worse			
Social Prestige						
London E.P.A.	25	34	41	100	127	18
Birmingham E.P.A.	22	48	31	100	65	5
West Riding E.P.A.	27	44	29	100	45	14
Security						
London E.P.A.	58	37	5	100	129	16
Birmingham E.P.A.	64	35	2	100	66	4
West Riding E.P.A.	57	35	9	100	46	13
Intellectual Stimulation						
London E.P.A.	48	27	25	100	127	18
Birmingham E.P.A.	45	41	14	100	66	4
West Riding E.P.A.	57	17	26	100	46	13
Social Stimulation						
London E.P.A.	26	28	46	100	127	18
Birmingham E.P.A.	28	37	35	100	65	5
West Riding E.P.A.	20	30	50	100	46	13
Neighbourhood in which you Work						
London E.P.A.	5	8	87	100	126	19
Birmingham E.P.A.	8	9	83	100	65	5
West Riding E.P.A.	2	24	74	100	46	13
Physical Conditions						
London E.P.A.	13	18	68	100	126	19
Birmingham E.P.A.	6	16	78	100	64	6
West Riding E.P.A.	13	30	57	100	46	13
Pressure of Work						
London E.P.A.	13	25	62	100	127	18
Birmingham E.P.A.	9	30	61	100	66	4
West Riding E.P.A.	11	18	70	100	44	15
Volume and Hours of Work						
London E.P.A.	44	21	35	100	128	17
Birmingham E.P.A.	47	29	24	100	66	4
West Riding E.P.A.	31	16	53	100	45	14
Present Salary						
London E.P.A.	16	15	69	100	129	16
Birmingham E.P.A.	22	17	62	100	65	5
West Riding E.P.A.	17	20	63	100	46	13
Salary Scale as a Whole						
London E.P.A.	9	14	77	100	127	18
Birmingham E.P.A.	18	14	68	100	65	5
West Riding E.P.A.	20	7	73	100	45	14
Position as a Whole (including Salary)						
London E.P.A.	13	23	64	100	125	20
Birmingham E.P.A.	21	29	50	100	66	4
West Riding E.P.A.	16	33	51	100	45	14

Table B.16 continued

	% giving response			Total %	Total no. respondents	No. non-respondents
	better	same	worse			
Position as a Whole *(excluding Salary)*						
London E.P.A.	28	34	38	100	122	23
Birmingham E.P.A.	24	42	33	100	66	4
West Riding E.P.A.	29	31	40	100	45	14
Opportunities to Improve *Qualifications*						
London E.P.A.	49	29	22	100	124	21
Birmingham E.P.A.	50	32	18	100	66	4
West Riding E.P.A.	39	26	35	100	46	13
General Satisfaction						
London E.P.A.	61	29	10	100	125	20
Birmingham E.P.A.	54	38	8	100	65	5
West Riding E.P.A.	58	29	13	100	45	14

Table B.17

Teachers' comparisons of their teaching situation with that of teachers they know in other schools, by project area

	% giving response			Total %	Total no. respondents	No. non-respondents
	better	same	worse			
Intellectual Stimulation						
London E.P.A.	24	39	37	100	124	21
Birmingham E.P.A.	15	39	46	100	67	3
West Riding E.P.A.	29	37	35	100	49	10
Social Stimulation						
London E.P.A.	33	36	32	100	123	22
Birmingham E.P.A.	21	36	43	100	67	3
West Riding E.P.A.	22	35	43	100	49	10
Discipline in the Classroom						
London E.P.A.	18	33	49	100	124	21
Birmingham E.P.A.	22	35	43	100	68	2
West Riding E.P.A.	32	50	18	100	50	9
Support from Parents						
London E.P.A.	17	29	54	100	125	20
Birmingham E.P.A.	2	18	80	100	65	5
West Riding E.P.A.	25	31	43	100	51	8
Pressure of Work						
London E.P.A.	10	42	48	100	126	19
Birmingham E.P.A.	7	57	36	100	67	3
West Riding E.P.A.	14	48	38	100	50	9
Volume and Hours of Work						
London E.P.A.	10	58	32	100	124	21
Birmingham E.P.A.	5	68	27	100	66	4
West Riding E.P.A.	12	52	36	100	50	9

Table B.17 continued

	% giving response better	same	worse	Total %	Total no. respondents	No. non-respondents
Physical Conditions of Work						
London E.P.A.	17	31	52	100	126	19
Birmingham E.P.A.	9	9	82	100	67	3
West Riding E.P.A.	22	16	62	100	50	9
Neighbourhood in which you Work						
London E.P.A.	3	12	85	100	127	18
Birmingham E.P.A.	1	3	96	100	67	3
West Riding E.P.A.	2	24	75	100	51	8
Teaching Facilities and Equipment						
London E.P.A.	38	34	29	100	125	20
Birmingham E.P.A.	15	34	51	100	67	3
West Riding E.P.A.	24	35	41	100	51	8
Recognition of Work by the Community at Large						
London E.P.A.	15	43	43	100	122	23
Birmingham E.P.A.	16	15	69	100	62	8
West Riding E.P.A.	22	41	37	100	49	10
Worthwhileness of the Work						
London E.P.A.	67	27	6	100	125	20
Birmingham E.P.A.	67	30	3	100	66	4
West Riding E.P.A.	74	20	6	100	50	9
The Ability of the Children you Teach						
London E.P.A.	5	21	75	100	126	19
Birmingham E.P.A.	3	9	88	100	66	4
West Riding E.P.A.	10	27	63	100	51	8
General Satisfaction						
London E.P.A.	51	34	15	100	125	20
Birmingham E.P.A.	39	50	11	100	66	4
West Riding E.P.A.	47	45	8	100	49	10

Relationship of job satisfaction to age and sex

There were, as we have just shown, strong relationships between a teacher's satisfaction with various aspects of his job and the project area in which he taught, relationships which seem to be better explained by the characteristics of the project areas and project schools than by the different age structures of the teaching staff in them. However, in exploring the relationship between job satisfaction and the personal characteristics of teachers these differences between areas inevitably became confused with differences in age and experience, so that it was difficult to disentangle the separate effects of each. Thus it was only possible to examine this relationship within each area, rather than using the pooled data from all three, and the London project area was the only one which had sufficient numbers of teachers to make the appropriate cross-tabulations meaningful.

In making this analysis of the London results the same method was adopted as had been used in the analysis of teachers' attitudes. Cross-tabulations were formed between each pairing of biographical variables with the comparisons made by teachers, and the probability level of the associated χ^2 was assessed. A probability of less than ·05 was taken not as a test of the significance of the relationship (for we did not have a random sample of teachers), but as a simple and objective criterion of its importance.

Using this criterion, virtually no relationships were found between teachers' personal characteristics and comparisons of their teaching situation with that of teachers in other schools. This absence of correlations is interesting in itself, for it means that dissatisfaction with the teaching situation in the London project schools is likely to be felt by all types of teacher, whether they be young and newly arrived at the school or middle-aged and with several years of service. It therefore further suggests that the dissatisfaction is due to objective problems in the schools, and not simply the teachers' subjective perceptions of the situation.

The attractiveness of teaching as compared with the jobs of friends depended, predictably, on two main factors, age and sex. The different views of men and women are set out in Table B.18, and clearly reflect the different standards which they have in mind when making the comparisons. Women's jobs have generally lower prestige and lower pay than men's, so it is not surprising that in comparing themselves with friends they were more satisfied than men in these respects—though even among women more thought they were worse off than thought they were better off. In contrast, more men than women felt they were better off than their friends in the security and intellectual stimulation which their job offered, and presumably these were major reasons why they chose to enter the profession. In assessing their position as a whole excluding salary, the views of men were more polarised than those of women but the majority of men still thought they were worse off, and while two-thirds of women said that their job afforded more general satisfaction than other jobs, only 39 per cent of men agreed with them.

Table B.18

Differences between men and women teachers in the London project schools in their comparisons of their jobs with the jobs of friends of approximately the same age and with equivalent qualifications

		% giving response			Total %	Total no. respondents	Total non-respondents
		better	same	worse			
Social Prestige	Men	21	21	59	100	29	2
	Women	27	38	35	100	97	16
Security	Men	76	21	3	100	29	2
	Women	52	42	5	100	99	14
Intellectual Stimulation	Men	71	18	11	100	28	3
	Women	41	30	30	100	98	15
Present Salary	Men	10	0	90	100	29	2
	Women	18	19	63	100	99	14
Position as a Whole	Men	32	11	57	100	28	3
(excluding Salary)	Women	26	42	32	100	93	20
General Satisfaction	Men	39	36	25	100	28	3
	Women	67	27	6	100	96	17

Table B.19 shows those aspects of job satisfaction which distinguish older and younger teachers. Not surprisingly, as teachers' salaries are on an incremental scale, teachers in their twenties were more dissatisfied with their present salary than older teachers, though a majority of both age groups thought they were worse off than friends. Younger teachers were also more dissatisfied with the salary scale as a whole, though again a large majority of both groups felt they were in a bad position in this respect. Finally, younger teachers were generally less content with the opportunities to improve their qualifications, which was clearly a matter of more importance to them than to their older colleagues.

Table B.19

Differences between older and younger teachers in the London project schools in their comparisons of their jobs with the jobs of friends of approximately the same age and with equivalent qualifications

| | | % giving response | | | Total % | Total no. respondents | No. non-respondents |
		better	same	worse			
Present Salary	Age below 30	11	10	79	100	63	6
	Age 30 or more	22	20	58	100	65	10
Salary Scale as	Age below 30	3	10	87	100	63	6
a Whole	Age 30 or more	14	19	67	100	63	12
Opportunities to	Age below 30	45	24	31	100	62	7
Improve Qualifications	Age 30 or more	54	34	12	100	61	14

Comparison with job satisfaction in non-E.P.A. samples

The questions on job satisfaction were originally used in the study of probationary teachers carried out by Bristol University Institute of Education, and data from two surveys which formed part of the programme of research was kindly made available to us for comparison. The first of these was a postal survey of a national sample of probationary teachers in half of the maintained primary and secondary schools in England and Wales.[1] It was conducted in two stages, and the questions on job satisfaction, which involved comparisons with the jobs of friends only, were included in the second stage at the end of the probationary year in the summer term of 1967. 3,588 teachers, 37 per cent of the sample, responded, of whom 2,148 taught in primary schools. The low response rate almost certainly meant that the sample was biassed, though we cannot say in what direction the bias operated.

There were just over 40 probationary teachers in the E.P.A. survey, not really enough to allow comparison with the probationary primary school teachers in the national survey. However, the opinions of the E.P.A. probationers were very similar to those of their more experienced colleagues: only on one item—present salary—was there a difference of more than 6 per cent between the two groups in the proportion thinking their job was worse than that of friends. Thus we were able to draw virtually the same conclusions from comparisons of the national sample with either group.

---

[1] J. K. Taylor and I. R. Dale, *A National Survey of Teachers in their First Year of Service*, University of Bristol, 1971.

We found that on all items but one, volume and hours of work, more of the E.P.A. teachers than of the national sample of probationary teachers considered they were worse off than friends in other jobs. The difference was greatest by far in respect of neighbourhood of work, with 84 per cent of E.P.A. teachers (89 per cent of E.P.A. probationers) saying they were worse off, compared with 32 per cent of the national sample. The E.P.A. teachers were also much more likely than the national sample to complain about social prestige, physical conditions, salary scale as a whole, and position as a whole excluding salary, on which items there was a difference of 20 per cent or more between the proportions in the two samples thinking their job worse.

The second survey was conducted as part of an action programme involving probationary teachers in four local education authorities: Bristol, Wolverhampton, Southwark and Devon.[1] The programme ran for three years, starting in 1968, and during the last two years special induction courses were organised. As part of the evaluation of the courses each cohort of probationers was asked at the end of the school year to complete the questions on job satisfaction, and the responses of the first two cohorts were kindly made available to us for comparison with the E.P.A. figures.

The questionnaire was distributed to all probationary teachers identified in the local education authority lists via the headteachers of their schools, and returned by post directly to the research team. In Southwark there was a total of 387 probationers in the two years, and of these 56 per cent responded. The rate in Wolverhampton, the other local authority of interest to us, was rather better: there 75 per cent of the 252 probationers in the two years completed the questionnaire. Although some teachers in the second year's cohort had attended special induction programmes, there were no significant differences between the responses of the second cohort and those of the previous one. Thus we felt justified in aggregating the figures for the two years.

The study asked teachers both to compare their job with the jobs of friends, and to compare their teaching situation with that of teachers in other schools. On the latter set of questions we compared the assessments of teachers in project schools in London, which were all situated of course in Deptford, with those of probationers in primary schools in the adjacent borough of Southwark, and the assessments of teachers in project schools in Birmingham with those of probationary primary school teachers in the neighbouring town of Wolverhampton. Obviously there were too few probationary teachers in the project schools in either area to treat as a separate group, but it will be remembered that the age and experience of E.P.A. teachers had virtually no bearing on their comparisons with teachers in other schools,[2] and hence we felt this would not invalidate the comparison.

The details of the comparisons are shown in Figures B(11) and B(12). The Borough of Southwark is similar in many respects to Deptford and has a number of E.P.A. schools of its own. However as the project schools were among those in Deptford which had the greatest difficulties we still expected the teachers there to be more dissatisfied than teachers in Southwark. This proved correct: there were more complaints from the teachers in the project schools about all aspects of their teaching situation with the exception of

---

[1] R. Bolam, *Experimental Induction Programmes for Probationary Teachers,* University of Bristol, 1973.

[2] See page 59 above.

teaching facilities and equipment, in which the project schools were known to be quite well off, and general satisfaction. The biggest differences between the two groups of teachers were in respect of pressure of work, neighbourhood and ability of the children.

Unlike Southwark, Wolverhampton is a town which has some E.P.A. schools but also some prosperous suburban districts. There was therefore a much greater contrast between the views of teachers in the project schools in Birmingham and probationary teachers in primary schools in Wolverhampton. Ninety-six per cent of the teachers in the project schools thought the

Figure B(11): Percentage of teachers in the London project schools who think their teaching situation is worse in various respects than that of teachers they know in other schools, compared with the corresponding percentage of all probationary teachers in primary schools in Southwark.

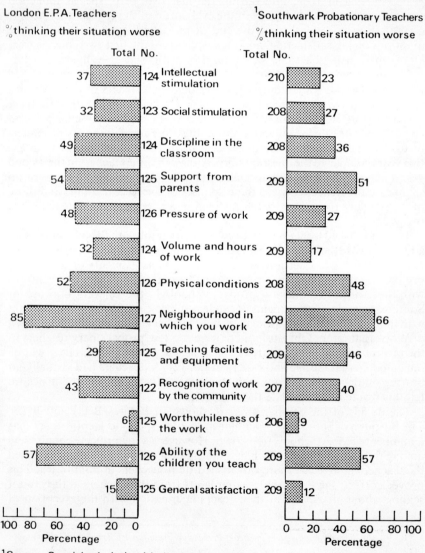

London E.P.A. Teachers
% thinking their situation worse

[1] Southwark Probationary Teachers
% thinking their situation worse

	Total No.			Total No.	
37	124	Intellectual stimulation	210		23
32	123	Social stimulation	208		27
49	124	Discipline in the classroom	208		36
54	125	Support from parents	209		51
48	126	Pressure of work	209		27
32	124	Volume and hours of work	209		17
52	126	Physical conditions	208		48
85	127	Neighbourhood in which you work	209		66
29	125	Teaching facilities and equipment	209		46
43	122	Recognition of work by the community	207		40
6	125	Worthwhileness of the work	206		9
57	126	Ability of the children you teach	209		57
15	125	General satisfaction	209		12

100 80 60 40 20 0
Percentage

0 20 40 60 80 100
Percentage

[1] Source: Special tabulation kindly made available by the Research Unit of Bristol University Institute of Education.

Figure B(12): Percentage of teachers in the Birmingham project schools who think that their teaching situation is worse in various respects than that of teachers they know in other schools, compared with the corresponding percentage of all probationary teachers in primary schools in Wolverhampton.

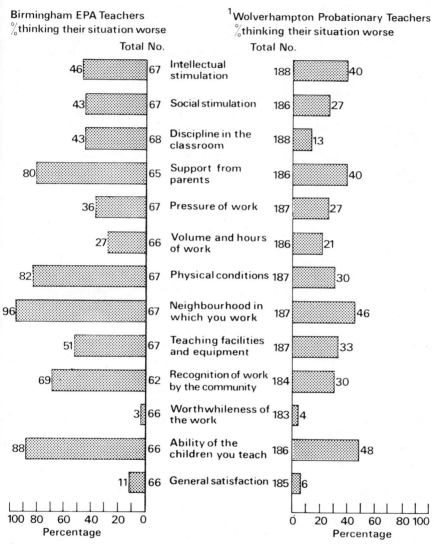

Birmingham EPA Teachers
%thinking their situation worse

[1]Wolverhampton Probationary Teachers
%thinking their situation worse

[1]Source: Special tabulation kindly made available by the Research Unit of Bristol University Institute of Education.

neighbourhood in which they worked was worse than for other teachers, compared with 46 per cent of the Wolverhampton probationers; 82 per cent complained of the physical conditions, compared with 30 per cent in Wolverhampton; and there were similarly large differences in the numbers complaining about support from parents, discipline in the classroom, recognition of work by the community, and the ability of the pupils. Only in the worthwhileness of the work did fewer of the project school teachers think they were worse off.

The comparisons of the E.P.A. and non-E.P.A. samples clearly show that teachers in the project schools were far more likely to see their position in an unfavourable light. As the straightforward analysis of the job satisfaction questions has already suggested, they found compensation primarily in the worthwhileness of the work and the general satisfaction which it gave.

Relationships among various aspects of job satisfaction

The contrast between views on the worthwhileness and general satisfaction of teaching in an E.P.A. school and the teachers' dissatisfaction with many other aspects of the work caused us to wonder what general satisfaction was associated with, and indeed what the relationships were among the various other aspects of job satisfaction. In order to investigate this, we calculated the matrix of associations within each set of comparisons, with friends and with teachers in other schools, using a measure of association between ordered classifications, Goodman and Kruskal's gamma.[1] The seven original response categories, from "very much better" to "very much worse", were used in the calculation, rather than the three summary categories "better", "same" and "worse", and so that numbers would be large enough for the analysis teachers in the Liverpool project schools were included, as also were teachers in Dundee project schools who have been excluded from every other analysis reported in this section.[2] There was an 81 per cent response rate to the survey of teachers in Dundee, and the inclusion of the Dundee and Liverpool teachers brought the total sample up to 380, with respondents to the individual items in the comparisons numbering between 318 and 342.

The two matrices of associations are given in Tables B.20 and B.21. Some patterns in the relationships among the variables are immediately visible: for instance, in Table B.21 "worthwhileness of work" has a high association only with "general satisfaction", and very small or even negative associations with everything else. In Table B.20 we see that "present salary" and "salary scale as a whole" have high associations with each other, and with "position as a whole including salary"; they also have a moderate degree of association with "social prestige" but their associations with other variables tend to be quite small. However, while patterns can be discerned by a close examination of the matrices, they are too complex to be completely elicited in this way. Some method is needed which will summarise the main relationships among the variables and present them in a way which makes it possible to assimilate them.

We therefore subjected the two matrices to the technique of analysis known as multidimensional scaling, a method of constructing a configuration of points in space from information about the distances between the points which can be applied to non-metric data.[3] Each aspect of job satisfaction— social prestige, security etc.—was regarded as a point, and the gamma coefficients as measures of the similarity or closeness between the points. Negative coefficients, which were all very small, were treated as though they represented greater distances between points than positive coefficients. We

---

[1] Gamma is a measure of association between classifications for each of which the set of classes or categories represents a directed ordering. In the words of its authors, "Gamma tells us how much more probable it is to get like than unlike orders in the two classifications, when two individuals are chosen at random from the population which has been classified". See L. A. Goodman and W. H. Kruskal, "Measures of association for cross-classification", *Journal of the American Statistical Association*, Vol. 49, 1954, pp. 732–763.

[2] For explanation see the Preface.

[3] For details of the method see R. N. Shepard, A. K. Romney and S. B. Nerlove, *Multidimensional Scaling*, Seminar Press, 1972. The analysis was performed by use of the computer program M-D-SCAL, Version 5M, written by J. B. Kruskal and F. Carmone.

Table B.20

Matrix of associations (gamma) among E.P.A. teachers' various comparisons of their jobs with the jobs of friends of the same age and with equivalent qualifications

Notes: Gamma has been calculated using the original seven response categories for each comparison, from "very much better" to "very much worse". The figures below the diagonal give the number of persons on which the corresponding coefficients are based. Numbers include teachers in Liverpool and Dundee project schools.

	Social prestige	Security	Intellectual stimulation	Social stimulation	Neighbourhood in which you work	Physical conditions	Pressure of work	Volume and hours of work	Present salary	Salary scale as a whole	Position as a whole (including salary)	Position as a whole (excluding salary)	Opp. to improve qualifications	General satisfaction
Social prestige		·33	·31	·36	·21	·26	·01	·08	·47	·47	·51	·52	·22	·22
Security	331		·32	·28	·08	·08	·03	·21	·11	·08	·17	·33	·26	·32
Intellectual stimulation	330	334		·48	·10	·13	·05	·02	·10	·04	·15	·33	·33	·36
Social stimulation	325	330	328		·22	·16	·07	·04	·16	·18	·18	·36	·21	·24
Neighbourhood in which you work	328	333	330	325		·48	·29	·14	·20	·25	·17	·24	·00	−·02
Physical conditions	323	329	326	321	326		·29	·11	·23	·23	·24	·23	·14	·00
Pressure of work	326	333	329	325	328	325		·52	·11	·11	·13	·14	·07	−·08
Volume and hours of work	327	333	330	325	329	326	329		·10	·09	·09	·19	·09	−·05
Present salary	326	332	329	324	328	324	327	329		·83	·79	·45	·31	·18
Salary scale as a whole	323	329	326	321	326	322	324	327	328		·80	·38	·21	·12
Position as a whole (including salary)	325	329	328	322	326	322	324	327	326	326		·60	·34	·29
Position as a whole (excluding salary)	321	325	324	318	322	318	320	323	322	322	325		·29	·34
Opp. to improve qualifications	324	330	327	322	327	323	325	327	327	325	325	323		·38
General satisfaction	323	328	326	321	325	321	323	325	325	323	324	321	327	

Table B.21

Matrix of associations (gamma) among E.P.A. teachers' various comparisons of their teaching situation with that of teachers they know in other schools

Notes: Gamma has been calculated using the original seven response categories for each comparison, from "very much better" to "very much worse". The figures below the diagonal give the number of persons on which the corresponding coefficients are based. Numbers include teachers in Liverpool and Dundee project schools.

	Intellectual stimulation	Social stimulation	Discipline in the classroom	Support from parents	Pressure of work	Volume and hours of work	Physical conditions	Neighbourhood in which you teach	Teaching facilities and equipment	Recognition of work by community	Worthwhileness of work	Ability of children you teach	General satisfaction
Intellectual stimulation		·55	·38	·29	·12	·10	·18	·31	·29	·28	·11	·25	·29
Social stimulation	331		·28	·30	·13	·08	·11	·22	·20	·27	·11	·19	·24
Discipline in the classroom	331	327		·47	·28	·07	·07	·26	·06	·27	·01	·36	·23
Support from parents	333	328	331		·36	·16	·30	·54	·27	·62	−·08	·54	·05
Pressure of work	337	331	335	337		·78	·30	·46	·14	·24	−·10	·39	·05
Volume and hours of work	334	329	332	335	339		·29	·39	·09	·17	−·23	·35	−·06
Physical conditions	338	332	335	338	342	339		·47	·51	·20	−·06	·29	·04
Neighbourhood in which you teach	338	332	336	339	342	339	342		·33	·40	−·27	·62	−·11
Teaching facilities	335	329	333	336	339	336	340	340		·23	·07	·23	·11
Recognition of work by community	322	318	319	327	326	323	327	327	325		·11	·36	·24
Worthwhileness of work	335	329	331	336	338	335	339	339	337	327		−·17	·63
Ability of children you teach	335	330	333	338	339	336	340	341	338	326	337		−·01
General satisfaction	333	328	329	334	336	333	337	337	334	324	335	338	

chose to represent the data in a three-dimensional space, which gave a meaningful configuration of points without losing too much information.

In multidimensional scaling the goodness of fit between the real and the projected distances between points is measured by the degree of stress. The fitted three-dimensional space for the set of comparisons with the jobs of friends had stress 15 per cent, and for comparisons with teachers in other schools, 17 per cent,[1] both of which represent a fit which is by convention considered fair to good.

Figures B(13) and B(14) plot the configuration of points for the comparisons with friends and comparisons with other schools in a three-dimensional space which has been constructed from the two matrices of associations. The reader should imagine he is looking at a two-dimensional plane with a third dimension passing vertically through the centre. The location of the various aspects of job satisfaction in this space is defined by their scores on the three dimensions and shown by the tips of the arrows. Distance between points in this space is inverse to the degree of association between them, so that where points are close together they represent a highly inter-correlated group.

Figure B(13): Representation in three-dimensional space of the similarities among various aspects of the E.P.A. teachers' satisfaction when comparing themselves with friends in other jobs

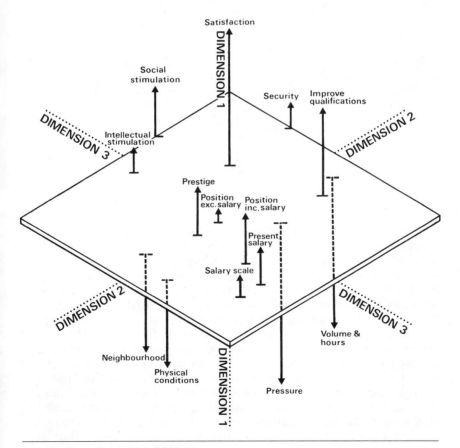

[1] Using Formula 2 in M-D-SCAL.

Figure B(14): Representation in three-dimensional space of the similarities among various aspects of the E.P.A. teachers' satisfaction when comparing themselves with teachers in other schools

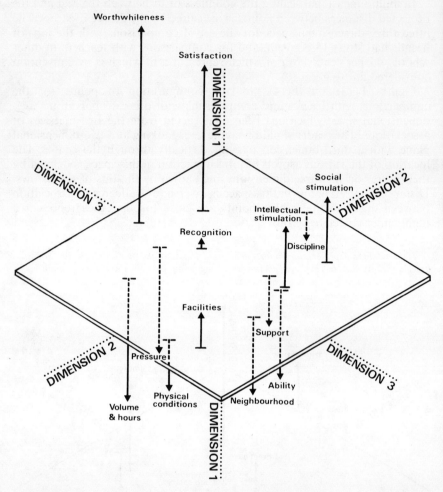

In Figure B(13) we can pick out several such groups among aspects of satisfaction with teaching as a job compared with other jobs. Present salary, salary scale and position as a whole including salary form one, which is not very far distant from prestige and position as a whole excluding salary. Neighbourhood and physical conditions are closely related and quite separated from other aspects, as are social and intellectual stimulation. Security and the opportunity to improve qualifications are closer together than they are to anything else, but still relatively far apart, and the same applies to pressure of work and volume and hours of work. General satisfaction stands very much by itself, but more closely associated with other psychological rewards—social stimulation, intellectual stimulation and prestige—and with security and the opportunity to improve qualifications, than with either the amount and intensity of work demanded or the neighbourhood and physical conditions of work, which appear to have very little relevance to general satisfaction. It is, however, associated slightly more closely with satisfaction with salary levels. In contrast, position as a whole excluding salary is much more closely related to prestige and considerations of salary than it is to other psychological rewards.

The representation of aspects of satisfaction with the particular teaching situation in Figure B(14) shows even more strikingly the independence of general satisfaction from most other aspects. It is associated at all closely only with the worthwhileness of the work, which itself is even less related to other aspects. Intellectual stimulation and social stimulation are again more closely related to general satisfaction than other aspects, though they are still some considerable distance away. A further cluster of inter-related factors, neighbourhood, support from parents and ability of the children, all reflect views about the population served by the school, and neither discipline nor recognition of work by the community are very far from this group. Finally, volume and hours of work and pressure of work appear fairly close together, and not too far away are physical conditions and teaching facilities and equipment.

We may conclude therefore that the general satisfaction of E.P.A. teachers with both teaching as a profession compared with others and with their particular situation depends primarily on the psychological rewards it brings and not on the easiness or pleasantness of the work. Salary has some bearing on it too, and it seems as though improvements in salary would be more likely to increase both general satisfaction and satisfaction with position as a whole relative to other groups than would improvements in other non-psychological aspects of the job. However though this might induce teachers to stay in the profession, it would not necessarily persuade them to remain in the inner city project schools which suffer seriously from high teacher turnover.

Appendix to Section B

Questionnaire used in the E.P.A. Project's Survey of Teachers

Note: In the attitude questions (pages 71 to 73) the scale to which each item belongs is given, and the scored response is underlined, or, in the case of scale G, the direction of scoring is indicated. This information did not appear in the version of the questionnaire which was distributed to teachers.

OPINIONS OF TEACHERS IN PRIMARY SCHOOLS

The questionnaire which follows is designed to give us a frank expression of your opinions about various aspects of teaching in primary schools. It consists of a number of statements which have been made by teachers. We should like you to indicate your *own personal* degree of agreement or disagreement with each of these statements by circling the appropriate letters which appear after each statement. The letters are:—

> SA = "Strongly Agree"
> A = "Agree"
> N = "Neutral" or "Undecided"
> D = "Disagree"
> SD = "Strongly Disagree"

Please circle only *one* of these categories for each statement. We should like your views as a practising teacher, bearing in mind your previous experience and your present school and class. *Would you please not discuss the statements with anybody before you have finished.*

The statements are controversial so there are no right or wrong answers. People do of course differ in their opinions and this questionnaire is intended to give some indication of how your opinions compare with those of other people. Your responses will be treated as strictly *confidential* and *no reference to individuals will be made in any report.*

We do not need your name but please underline the categories below which describe you.

Age	*Sex*	*Type of School*	*Region*
25 and under	Male	Infant	Birmingham
26–35	Female	Primary (including Infants)	Dundee
35 and over		Primary (excluding Infants)	Liverpool
			London
			West Riding
			Other

		Strongly Agree	Agree	Neutral	Disagree	Strongly Disagree
A	1. It is good for a school if both the teachers and the children live in the local area.	SA	A	N	D	SD
C	2. Disadvantaged children come from poor degenerate stock, there is nothing much you can do about it educationally.	SA	A	N	D	SD
G	3. Less able children can generally be relied upon to do a job faithfully.	4 SA	A	N	D	0 SD
B	4. Most parents exaggerate the abilities and virtues of their own children.	SA	A	N	D	SD
A	5. Teachers should be willing to visit problem families occasionally out of school hours.	SA	A	N	D	SD
A	6. Teachers should accept positions of leadership in the community.	4 SA	A	N	D	0 SD
G	7. Teaching backward children is interesting.	SA	A	N	D	SD
E	8. Physical punishment does no good at all to any child.	SA	A	N	D	SD
B	9. Parents should continually be encouraged to discuss their children's progress with teachers.	SA	A	N	D	SD
A	10. School children should pay fairly frequent visits to local firms and places of interest.	SA	A	N	D	SD
C	11. Disadvantaged children should be given a free holiday every year at the ratepayer's expense.	SA	A	N	D	SD
G	12. I would find teaching the backward the least rewarding job in a primary school.	0 SA	A	N	D	4 SD
B	13. Many parents couldn't care less about their child's school life and it is not part of the teacher's job to persuade them to care.	SA	A	N	D	SD
C	14. Deprived children should be taught in smaller classes than others even though this may raise the cost of education.	SA	A	N	D	SD
F	15. There is too much emphasis on cutting down noise in schools.	SA	A	N	D	SD
B	16. If I am teaching in a school which has a parent-teacher association I do my best to avoid the meetings.	SA	A	N	D	SD
A	17. The morale of a school depends as much on the neighbourhood from which it draws its children as on the headteacher and teachers.	SA	A	N	D	SD
A	18. Every school should have close relations with the local newspaper.	SA	A	N	D	SD
C	19. Deprived children should be taught by teachers specially chosen for their interest and sympathy.	SA	A	N	D	SD
F	20. I don't mind a reasonably high working noise in my class.	SA	A	N	D	SD
A	21. Teachers should use their special knowledge to help social workers in the community.	SA	A	N	D	SD
C	22. There is too much talk about underprivileged children and not enough about the taxpayer.	SA	A	N	D	SD
C	23. Extra provision of staff and equipment should be made so that children in poor areas can have after-school activities.	SA	A	N	D	SD
F	24. I would not allow talking in a class of 35 or more children.	SA	A	N	D	SD
C	25. It is wasteful to spend extra money and energy on children who are unlikely to do anything but unskilled manual labour.	SA	A	N	D	SD
G	26. Less able children are often outstanding in art or drama.	4 SA	A	N	D	0 SD
E	27. If children in my class are insolent they have to be slapped.	SA	A	N	D	SD

		Strongly Agree	Agree	Neutral	Disagree	Strongly Disagree
C	28. Special help for educationally deprived children is money down the drain.	SA 4	A	N	D	SD 0
G	29. Slow children gain much from a free-activity approach.	SA	A	N	D	SD
E	30. An occasional hard slap does children no harm.	SA	A	N	D	SD
B	31. Many parents try to meddle too much in their child's education.	SA	A	N	D	SD
D	32. Teachers should demand clean hands in school.	SA	A	N	D	SD
A	33. I have better things to do with my time than helping to solve local problems.	SA	A	N	D	SD
D	34. I cannot stand fidgeting in class.	SA	A	N	D	SD
B	35. Every school should have an open day to discuss their objectives with the parents.	SA	A	N	D	SD
E	36. I think a good slap in the right place at the right time does an awful lot of good.	SA	A	N	D	SD
C	37. Children from poor homes should receive special encouragement and help from their teachers.	SA	A	N	D	SD
D	38. Naturalness is more important than good manners in children.	SA	A	N	D	SD
A	39. Schools are for teaching children academic subjects; there is too strong a tendency nowadays to turn them into social centres.	SA	A	N	D	SD
B	40. I don't want parents telling me what to do with their child in school.	SA	A	N	D	SD
C	41. Everything possible should be done educationally to compensate children from poor homes.	SA	A	N	D	SD
D	42. Opportunities for self-expression through movement, painting and writing poetry are more important than concentrating on the "three Rs".	SA	A	N	D	SD
E	43. I'm quite prepared to spank bottoms for disobeying rules.	SA	A	N	D	SD
A	44. At least one way in which country schools excel over town schools is that they are more a part of the community.	SA 0	A	N	D	SD 4
G	45. The majority of less able children have no interest in school.	SA	A	N	D	SD
A	46. School teachers are naturally the leaders of any community.	SA	A	N	D	SD
B	47. I always find it helpful and enlightening to have a talk with parents and only the occasional one is difficult.	SA	A	N	D	SD
F	48. Nothing worthwhile will be achieved by a class that talks while it works.	SA	A	N	D	SD
B	49. A report once each term is sufficient communication between teachers and parents.	SA	A	N	D	SD
C	50. Children from poor homes should be given special opportunities to take part in after-school activities.	SA	A	N	D	SD
E	51. Physical punishment is out of the question and completely unnecessary.	SA	A	N	D	SD
B	52. Most parents are pretty reasonable about their children's school problems.	SA	A	N	D	SD
F	53. A quiet atmosphere is the one best suited for all school work.	SA	A	N	D	SD
A	54. Local "leading citizens" should not be encouraged to offer their opinions on the affairs of a school.	SA	A	N	D	SD
B	55. If the parents want to know anything about the children in my class I prefer them to discuss it with the headteacher and not with me.	SA	A	N	D	SD

		Strongly Agree	Agree	Neutral	Disagree	Strongly Disagree
A	56. Teachers have no special obligation in the community apart from doing their job in the school.	SA	A	N	D	SD
		4				0
G	57. I would enjoy the challenge of teaching less able children.	SA	A	N	D	SD
D	58. Children must be taught to have decent manners.	SA	A	N	D	SD
B	59. It should be made clear that parents have no say in any punishment which their child receives at school, provided that it is legal.	SA	A	N	D	SD
C	60. It is not fair to other children to spend money on areas designated as educationally deprived.	SA	A	N	D	SD
B	61. Teachers and parents are responsible for quite different aspects of the child and they should not interfere with each other.	SA	A	N	D	SD
C	62. Children from the worst areas should be given the best schools to make up for their backgrounds.	SA	A	N	D	SD

1. What is the full name and address of your school?

2. Please indicate your sex and marital status:

Single Woman	
Single Man	
Married Woman	
Married Man	
Widow	
Widower	

3. Please indicate your age:

Under 25	
25–29	
30–34	
35–39	
40–44	
45–49	
50–54	
55–59	
60 or over	

4. (a) Into which of the following categories does/did your father's occupation fall?

Professional, administrative	
Managerial, executive	
Clerical, supervisory	
Skilled manual	
Semi-skilled manual	
Unskilled manual	
Teacher	

    (b) What is your country of origin?

5. Please indicate the nature of your qualification for teaching:

Certificate of Education (2 year course)

Certificate of Education (3 year course)

Degree and Postgraduate Certificate

Degree only

Unqualified

6. Which year did you obtain your qualification for teaching?

19

7. For how many years have you been teaching altogether? (Those with broken service e.g. military or family commitments should count only the actual number of years taught.)

Years

8. How long have you been teaching in this school?

Years

9. What position do you hold in the school?

10. Please give details, as accurately as you can, of the teaching posts you held before coming to this school:

e.g.

Date	Type of school	Position
1953–57	Bridge Infant, Bristol	Assistant Teacher
1957–59	Bridge Infant, Bristol	Scale 1 allowance for reading
1959–63	Bridge Infant, Bristol	Deputy Head
1963	Greenacres J. M. and I., Leeds	In charge of Infant Department

Date	Name and Type of School	Position held

11. Please give details of any jobs held outside teaching which you have held for at least six months:

From	To	Job

12. About how far from the school do you live?

Less than $\frac{1}{2}$ mile	
1 to 2 miles[1]	
2 to 3 miles	
3 to 5 miles	
More than 5 miles	

13. How long does it take you to travel to school in the morning?

Less than $\frac{1}{4}$ hour	
$\frac{1}{4}$ to $\frac{1}{2}$ hour	
$\frac{1}{2}$ to $\frac{3}{4}$ hour	
$\frac{3}{4}$ to 1 hour	

---

[1] Sic.

How do you think teaching compares with the jobs of friends of approximately the same age and with equivalent qualifications, in the following respects:

	Very much better	A good deal better	Slightly better	About the same	Slightly worse	A good deal worse	Very much worse
Social prestige							
Security							
Intellectual stimulation							
Social stimulation							
Neighbourhood in which you work							
Physical conditions of work							
Pressure of work							
Volume and hours of work							
Present salary							
Salary scale as a whole							
Position as a whole (including salary)							
Position as a whole (excluding salary)							
Opportunities to improve qualifications							
General satisfaction							

How do you think your teaching situation compares with that of teachers you know in other schools in the following respects:

	Very much better	A good deal better	Slightly better	About the same	Slightly worse	A good deal worse	Very much worse
Intellectual stimulation							
Social stimulation							
Discipline in the classroom							
Support from parents							
Pressure of work							
Volume and hours of work							
Physical conditions of work							
Neighbourhood in which you work							
Teaching facilities and equipment							
Recognition of work by the community at large							
Worthwhileness of work							
The ability of the children you teach							
General satisfaction							

SECTION C

The Survey of Parents

Design of the survey

The third element in the baseline study of the project schools was a survey of the parents of pupils carried out in the summer term of 1969. The survey was designed by Roger Dale under the general guidance of Alan Brimer, both acting in their capacity as consultants to the E.P.A. Project from the Research Unit of the Institute of Education at Bristol University. They were assisted by Margaret Davis, who also supervised the fieldwork.

The survey was designed to collect information on a variety of topics which were felt to be relevant to the child's progress at school, including the educational background of the home, parents' general attitudes towards education and their ambitions for their own child, their contacts with the school, and the help which they gave their child at home. It also examined the closeness of parents' ties with the local community, the extent of nursery school and playgroup provision and the age at which children started school, the particular problems which children experienced at school, and parents' criticisms of the schools. A number of questions were taken from the national survey of parents conducted for the Plowden Report,[1] some from a study of parental involvement in a London junior school carried out by Young and McGeeney,[2] and others were specially devised for the survey by Roger Dale and Margaret Davis.[3]

To assist in the development of the questionnaire a pilot survey was conducted among the parents of pupils at three primary schools in Bristol which had similar problems to those experienced by the project schools. School A was an infant school on a council housing estate, with fairly old school buildings and a number of problem families in the catchment area. School B was a junior with infants school which had a number of immigrant pupils. It served a district where housing conditions were poor and its own buildings were old. The catchment area of School C, a brand new junior school, comprised immigrant and slum clearance families from the city centre, some living in high rise blocks of flats. A random sample of a hundred pupils was drawn from the class registers of these schools, and interviews, generally with the mothers, were conducted during the last two weeks of April 1969. The completed schedules were studied and discussions held with interviewers, and as a result some ambiguities and duplications were removed from the questionnaire and categories established for the answers to some uncoded questions.

For the main survey a random sample of children was drawn from the registers of the project schools, and their addresses were obtained from

---

[1] *Children and their Primary Schools: A Report of the Central Advisory Council for Education (England), Vol. 2, Research and Surveys.* H.M.S.O., 1967.

[2] Michael Young and Patrick McGeeney, *Learning Begins at Home.* Routledge and Kegan Paul Ltd., 1968.

[3] A copy of the questionnaire is given in the Appendix to this section.

the same source. The procedure adopted gave all children an equal chance of selection, though this meant that the parents of large families were more likely to be selected than the parents of small families. If the brother or sister of a child who was already part of the sample was chosen, he was replaced by another child. The aim was to achieve 200 interviews in each project area, and so the overall sampling fraction in each area varied according to the total number of pupils in the project schools there. The sampling design also permitted the sampling fraction to vary between project schools within an area, so that schools could be more heavily sampled if information about parents was particularly needed to help the action teams set up programmes for parental involvement. Two infant schools and a junior school in London and an infant and a junior school in Birmingham were excluded from the survey altogether, either because the headteacher was unwilling to co-operate, or in order to concentrate interviews in schools where they were of especial interest. Table C.1 shows the number of schools in each project area which did take part.

Table C.1

Schools taking part in the survey of parents, by type and project area

	London	Birmingham	Liverpool	West Riding	Total
Infant	3	0	5	4	12
Junior with infants	3	4	5	2	14
Junior	3	0	6	4	13
Total	9	4	16	10	39

Replacement samples were also drawn in each school, and the intended procedure was to take a replacement when parents could not be contacted, but not if they refused to be interviewed. However there was some confusion in the instructions on this point and the procedure was not followed consistently in all areas; it is therefore not possible to say how many refusals were received overall. The number of interviews obtained in each area from the main and replacement samples is shown in Table C.2. Most replacements were taken in the London and Birmingham project schools,

Table C.2

Number of interviews achieved in the survey of parents

	London	Birmingham	Liverpool	West Riding	Total
Total no. of interviews achieved	204	181	191	195	771
No. of interviews achieved from main sample	173	140	183	189	685
% of main sample	86·5%	70·0%	91·5%	94·5%	85·6%
No. of interviews achieved from replacement sample	31	41	8	6	86
% of total achieved sample	15·2%	22·6%	4·2%	3·1%	11·2%

serving districts which, according to the 1966 Census, had a higher degree of population mobility than either the Liverpool or the West Riding project areas. The addresses given for pupils in the school records were thus more likely to be out of date, though the confusion over the replacement procedure also contributed to the differences between areas in the number of replacements. Thus in terms both of the coverage of project schools and of response rate the samples in Liverpool and the West Riding are more satisfactory than the samples in London and Birmingham.

The number of interviews achieved in each school as a percentage of the number on the school roll varied in London from 6 per cent to 19 per cent, in Birmingham from 5 per cent to 11 per cent, in Liverpool (where a uniform sampling fraction was used across schools) from 5 per cent to 8 per cent, and in the West Riding from 6 per cent to 13 per cent. In three of the areas therefore any estimates based on the survey of the proportion of parents having a certain characteristic are biassed towards the schools where the larger sampling fractions were used. It would have been theoretically possible to construct a system of weights to be attached to the figures for each school to correct this, but given that the replacement procedure had been followed inconsistently and that in London and Birmingham not all project schools had been surveyed it was concluded that the extra complications entailed by weighting would not be justified by a significant increase in the reliability of the estimates.

Fifty-two per cent of the selected children in the achieved sample were boys and 48 per cent girls, the proportions varying slightly across areas. In Table C.3 we give the percentage of selected children in each age group, which should be approximately equal in the seven to eight and nine to ten age groups, slightly smaller in the five to six group, and considerably smaller in the eleven plus group. In fact younger children were under-represented in Birmingham and slightly over-represented in London; in Liverpool and the West Riding where the samples were more satisfactory the proportions of children in each age group were as expected.

Table C.3
Age of selected children in the achieved sample

Age	London %	Birmingham %	Liverpool %	West Riding %	Total %
5–6 years	30	15	27	28	25
7–8 years	33	21	32	31	30
9–10 years	24	46	30	30	32
11 +	13	19	11	12	13
Total %	100	100	100	100	100
(N)	(204)	(181)	(191)	(195)	(771)

Interviews were conducted by professional interviewers at the homes of parents during June and July 1969. Where possible the selected child's natural mother or the person who acted as his mother was interviewed, but if she was not available the child's father was seen. Table C.4 shows the number of cases where this was so. A few children stayed more or less permanently with their grandparents, and in these instances the grandmother was interviewed. When we give figures for parents in the tables which follow this should be understood to mean the people who were interviewed, unless it is expressly stated that the table refers to the child's father or mother.

Table C.4
Relationship of person interviewed to selected child

	London No.	Birmingham No.	Liverpool No.	West Riding No.	Total No.
Natural mother	195	167	180	190	732
Step-mother or adopted mother	4	4	1	2	11
Grandmother	1	1	4	2	8
Father	1	6	6	0	13
No information	3	3	0	1	7
Total	204	181	191	195	771

The population served by the project schools

The survey showed large differences among the four areas in the nature of the population served by the project schools. According to Table C.5 the majority of mothers in both Liverpool and the West Riding had spent their childhood in the district where they lived at the time of the survey, compared with 28 per cent in London and only 10 per cent in Birmingham. Furthermore, over half the mothers in Birmingham and a quarter in London had been brought up outside the U.K. or Eire, compared with only 4 per cent in Liverpool and none at all in the West Riding. Immigrants living in the London project area were mostly from the West Indies, but in Birmingham they were divided fairly evenly between West Indians and Asians from India or Pakistan. For London, Liverpool and the West Riding the proportions of parents born abroad reflect very closely the figures in Table A.3 (page 7) giving the countries of origin of children taking the vocabulary

Table C.5
Place where selected child's mother was brought up, by project area

	London %	Birmingham %	Liverpool %	West Riding %
Same area	28	10	60	65
Same city* or within 5 mile radius†	8	14	24	11
Rest of Great Britain	25	10	9	21
Northern or Southern Ireland	12	9	2	3
All U.K. and Eire	*73*	*43*	*95*	*100*
West Indies	22	25	3	0
India or Pakistan	0	27	0	0
Elsewhere	4	3	1	0
All outside U.K. and Eire	*26*	*55*	*4*	*0*
No mother or no information	0	2	2	1
Total %	100	100	100	100
(N)	(204)	(181)	(191)	(195)

* If Liverpool or Birmingham.

† If London or the West Riding.

test, but in Birmingham the proportion of non-immigrants among the children tested was higher than the proportion of mothers from the U.K. or Eire in the survey of parents. There appeared in fact to be a higher proportion of West Indian mothers than West Indian children, which may have been a result of the biasses in the sampling, or which alternatively may have arisen because the mothers had been resident in this country for more than ten years so that their children born in this country were not classified as immigrants by the Department of Education and Science.

In tabulating information by country of origin in subsequent tables, families where at least one parent came from the West Indies were counted as West Indian, and families in which at least one parent came from India or Pakistan were counted as Asian. There were no mixed marriages with one West Indian and one Asian partner. These definitions, which are wider than those used by the D.E.S., were adopted in order to give sufficient numbers within each group to allow breakdowns to be made within it.

The fact that the Birmingham and to a lesser extent the London project areas were reception areas for families from abroad was reflected in a number of questions put together in Table C.6 which revealed what we might call a family's "vertical roots" in the area. Each of these questions— whether the parents were brought up in the same area or attended the same school as their child, how long they had lived in the same house, and where they had moved from if they had lived there less than five years—make it clear that the Liverpool and especially the West Riding project areas had very stable populations, while there was a high proportion of newcomers among the residents of the London and again more particularly the Birmingham project areas. When we look, however, in Table C.7 at the proximity of relatives and friends—what might be termed "horizontal roots" —differences between the areas, though still apparent, are much reduced. This no doubt reflects the understandable tendency of immigrant families to settle in districts to which their friends and relatives have moved before them, and shows how districts of high population mobility can nevertheless contain closely knit communities.

Table C.6

"Vertical roots" of families in the four project areas

Percentage of families in various categories

	London %	Birmingham %	Liverpool %	West Riding %
Child's mother was brought up in same area	28	10	60	65
Child's father was brought up in same area	27	4	57	69
Mother or father attended child's present school	9	2	25	25
Family lived in same house for 15 years or more	21	13	31	45
Family moved house less than 5 years ago, but previously lived within 1 mile of present address	15	1	22	25
Total number of families	(204)	(181)	(191)	(195)

Table C.7
"Horizontal roots" of families in the four project areas

Percentage of families in various categories

	London %	Birmingham %	Liverpool %	West Riding %
Many of mother's relatives live nearby	44	45	51	66
Many of father's relatives live nearby	33	46	45	62
Many of mother's and father's friends live nearby	50	56	58	86
Child plays with local children after school	77	76	90	95
Total number of families	(204)	(181)	(191)	(195)

In a number of interviews information about the father's occupation was missing or not classifiable. However the vast majority of fathers had manual occupations, with very roughly half in semi-skilled or unskilled jobs and half in skilled ones. As Table C.8 shows, employment opportunities for mothers were rather greater in London than elsewhere, and there was no significant difference in London between the proportions of working mothers in West Indian and U.K. and Eire families.[1] In Birmingham however almost twice as many mothers in West Indian families went out to work than in the U.K. and Eire group ($P < \cdot01$), and no Asian mothers worked at all.

Table C.8
Employment of mothers, by project area and family's country of origin

	No paid employment %	Part or full time paid employment %	No mother %	Total %	(N)
All London mothers	*52*	*48*	*0*	*100*	*(204)*
U.K. and Eire	50	50	0	100	(144)
West Indies	57	43	0	100	(47)
All Birmingham mothers	*67*	*32*	*1*	*100*	*(181)*
U.K. and Eire	64	35	1	100	(72)
West Indies	37	62	0	100	(48)
India and Pakistan	100	0	0	100	(52)
All Liverpool mothers	*61*	*39*	*1*	*100*	*(191)*
All West Riding mothers	*67*	*33*	*0*	*100*	*(195)*

[1] Although the parental survey sample cannot be regarded as a truly random one because of the confusion over the replacement procedure. χ^2 with one degree of freedom has been used within areas to test whether observed differences in the sample reflect differences in the total population of E.P.A. families in that area. Unless specified otherwise, a ·05 level of significance on a one-tailed test has been accepted. The reader may if he wishes disregard the reports of the significance tests.

Although family size varied considerably among areas and ethnic groups, most families in all the groups in Table C.9 were larger than the national average. West Riding families and London families of U.K. or Eire origin were the smallest, but even among them three-fifths had three or more children. How far the distribution of family size was affected by the sampling procedure we cannot say. Both West Indian and Asian families in Birmingham were significantly bigger than U.K. and Eire families there, and in London West Indian families were also significantly larger than families from the British Isles. The generally greater size of families in Birmingham when compared with the other areas was due in part to the fact that the parents of younger children were under-represented in the Birmingham sample, so that a higher proportion of the sampled parents in Birmingham had completed their families. There was no parallel explanation however for the variations in family size among ethnic groups, as the selected children had a very similar distribution of ages in each group.

Table C.9

Number of children in family, by project area and country of origin

| | Number of children | | | | | |
	1–2 %	3–4 %	5+ %	No information %	Total %	(N)
All London families	*31*	*39*	*30*	*0*	*100*	*(204)*
U.K. and Eire	40	35	25	0	100	(144)
West Indies	9	45	47	0	100	(47)
All Birmingham families	*9*	*36*	*55*	*0*	*100*	*(181)*
U.K. and Eire	19	29	51	0	100	(72)
West Indies	4	33	62	0	100	(48)
India and Pakistan	2	48	50	0	100	(52)
All Liverpool families	*19*	*43*	*37*	*1*	*100*	*(191)*
All West Riding families	*36*	*41*	*24*	*0*	*100*	*(195)*

Pre-school provision and starting school

The survey revealed marked discrepancies among the project areas in the availability of pre-school education. By far the best provision was made in the London project area, where 41 per cent of the sampled children had been to either nursery school or playgroup, compared with 26 per cent in Liverpool and only 4 per cent in the West Riding. In Birmingham the corresponding figure was 12 per cent, but half of these had attended abroad. These figures were not of course a direct measure of the level of provision in the four areas because of the families who had left or arrived after their child had completed pre-school; such movements however are unlikely to explain the very large differences between areas. In addition, the figures refer not to the level of provision at any one time, but to the average level over a period of seven or so years before the survey of parents was carried out. The E.P.A. project teams later helped to set up new groups which eased the situation to some extent.

The lack of nurseries and playgroups was made more serious by the fact that the pressure of numbers on the project schools had meant that many children were not able to start attending school mornings and afternoons until they were over five years old. Even if we exclude the children of immigrant parents who may not have arrived in this country until after the normal age for starting school, still 50 per cent of children in the London project schools, 52 per cent in Birmingham and 65 per cent in Liverpool did not start school until after the age of five. Only in the West Riding project schools was there relatively little pressure on places, and there, in line with the policy of the West Riding Education Authority, two-thirds of the sampled children started school before their fifth birthday. Over a third of parents in each project area said they would have liked their child to have started school earlier than he did, and the majority of these said they would have preferred him to start attending mornings and afternoons before he was four and a half. The reason given most often was that children were ready for school at that age, though several also mentioned that it would enable their child to mix with others, and a few that it would give themselves more free time.

The educational background of the home and ambitions for children

Table C.10 shows the ages at which the mothers of the sampled children had themselves left school. For the majority this was as early as possible, when they were 14 or 15, depending on the year. Only a handful of Liverpool and West Riding mothers and of mothers of U.K. and Eire origin in Birmingham had stayed on beyond the age of 15, though 16 per cent of U.K. and Eire mothers in London had done so.

In both London and Birmingham a significantly higher proportion of West Indian mothers than of U.K. or Eire mothers had stayed on at school beyond 15 years. Although we cannot say for certain that they had in fact received more years of full-time education, for they may have started school later or had intermittent periods of schooling, still the figures are consistent with the fact that the level of education among immigrants to this country from the West Indies was, at least during the early years, higher than that of the general population in their countries of origin.[1] In contrast, the majority of the mothers from India and Pakistan had not been to school at all, and of those who had, most left before they were 14 years old. The differences between the Asian group and the rest on this variable were statistically highly significant.

Information on father's education was less complete, but the same trends between project areas and ethnic groups were observed as described above.

The survey included a number of questions on parents' reading habits, the answers to which are set out in Table C.11. Although most families took either a local or a national daily newspaper, only a third took any kind of magazine or periodical. Two- to three-fifths of mothers in each project area said they liked to read books, but by this they often meant romantic story magazines, and very many fewer actually belonged to the local lending library. Over half the families in each project area did however possess a dictionary. The apparently lower popularity of reading on virtually all the measures in Birmingham as compared with the other areas arises because a number of the Asian mothers interviewed were illiterate.

---

[1] E. J. B. Rose and associates, *Colour and Citizenship: A Report on British Race Relations*. Oxford University Press, 1969, Chapter 5.

Table C.10
Age mother left school, by project area and country of origin

| | Age mother left school | | | | | | | |
	Did not go to school %	13 yrs. or younger %	14 yrs. %	15 yrs. %	16 yrs. or older %	No mother or no information %	Total %	(N)
All London families	0	7	30	43	20	0	*100*	*(204)*
U.K. and Eire	0	6	35	42	16	0	100	(144)
West Indies	0	2	13	49	34	2	100	(47)
All Birmingham families	17	11	30	25	13	4	*100*	*(181)*
U.K. and Eire	1	6	56	28	7	3	100	(69)
West Indies	0	4	17	46	29	4	100	(48)
India and Pakistan	52	27	6	6	4	6	100	(52)
All Liverpool families	1	1	43	50	5	1	*100*	*(191)*
All West Riding families	0	2	39	55	4	0	*100*	*(195)*

Table C.11
Educational background of the home, by project area
Percentage of families in various categories

	London %	Birmingham %	Liverpool %	West Riding %
Family takes at least one local daily newspaper	37	40	70	29
Family takes at least one national daily newspaper	85	46	69	87
Family takes at least one magazine or periodical	36	20	39	33
Parent likes to read books	67	42	40	44
Parent belongs to local lending library	18	8	5	21
Family possesses a dictionary	65	52	56	63
Total number of families	(204)	(181)	(191)	(195)

Despite their own relatively low level of education, a number of families were quite ambitious for their children. Only a tiny minority of parents thought that it was not very important for their child to do well at school, and between three-fifths and four-fifths in each project area thought it was "very important indeed". More than half in each project area believed their child was brighter than they were at the same age, and between 20 per cent and 30 per cent said specifically that they wanted their child to have a job which could be classed as semi-professional or professional—"a job with training" was a phrase often used. When asked at what age they would like their child to leave school (Table C.12) less than a third in each area— far fewer in London—gave the minimum leaving age, which in 1969 was 15, while at least a quarter in each—nearly half in London—said 18 years or older. In both London and Birmingham the West Indian parents were significantly more ambitious for their children than parents from the British Isles, with 57 per cent in London and 40 per cent in Birmingham wanting their child to stay on until he was at least 18. The preferences of the Asian parents were quite similar to those of the U.K. and Eire parents in Birmingham, though slightly more chose the minimum and the maximum ages and slightly fewer 16 or 17 years.

Table C.12

Age at which mothers would like their child to leave school, by project area and country of origin

| | *Preferred leaving age for child* | | | | | |
	Below 16 years %	16 or 17 years %	18 years or older %	No specific answer %	Total %	(N)
All London mothers	9	41	43	7	*100*	*(204)*
U.K. and Eire	11	43	37	8	100	(144)
West Indies	2	38	57	2	100	(47)
All Birmingham mothers	33	35	29	4	*100*	*(181)*
U.K. and Eire	35	39	21	6	100	(72)
West Indies	17	40	40	4	100	(48)
India and Pakistan	40	31	29	0	100	(52)
All Liverpool mothers	*31*	*41*	*25*	*3*	*100*	*(191)*
All West Riding mothers	*23*	*38*	*34*	*6*	*100*	*(195)*

Helping children at home

According to the answers to the questions listed in Table C.13, parents had fairly clear views on what their duties were as regards their children and what were the duties of the school. Controlling the child's behaviour was seen primarily as the parents' province: nearly two-thirds said it was the parents' job to teach children to keep off the streets and out of mischief, how to behave in public, and good manners. The school was held to have a slightly bigger part in moral instruction, for half of those interviewed thought it was the job of both parents and school to teach children the difference between right and wrong, though hardly any thought it was the school's job alone. On a very different dimension, 59 per cent felt it was the school's job and not the parents' to educate children so that they could get a good job, and also rather more said it was the school's job than said it was the parents' job to teach children a lot of interesting and useful things. As regards the social function of helping children to get to know other children, parents were fairly evenly divided between those who saw this as their job and those who felt it was the school's. A majority thought that both parents and school had a role in teaching children to talk properly, though of the remainder, more thought this was the parents' job than thought it was the school's. "Talking properly" is of course open to different interpretations, and it may be that parents were thinking of politeness rather than of grammatically correct speech.

It is not surprising in view of the fairly sharp line drawn by parents between their own duties and those of the school that a good proportion of children in each project area did not receive much help with their schoolwork. In Table C.14 we have put together the answers to a number of questions on this topic. Although the large majority of children talked to their parents about their work and showed them what they had been doing, only just over half of those interviewed (a quarter in Birmingham) knew what their child was doing at school at the moment, and only three-fifths—two-fifths in Birmingham—said they helped their child if he found difficulty with his work. The lower proportions in Birmingham are attributable to the Asian families there, who often, because of differences of culture and language, are unable to understand what their child does at school. In contrast the West Indian mothers, who had more years of schooling themselves and were more ambitious for their children, were more likely than mothers of U.K. or Eire origin to help their children with their schoolwork.

Table C.14 also gives an indication of the opportunities which children had for reading at home. Two-thirds of mothers in London and Liverpool and four-fifths in the West Riding said that their child had had at least one reading book bought for him during the previous twelve months, though the proportion in Birmingham was once more the lowest of the four. In addition, roughly half the children in London, Birmingham and the West Riding belonged to the public library, though strangely in Liverpool only 28 per cent did. However, only a quarter or so of mothers (10 per cent in Birmingham) helped their child to choose books.

Contacts between parents and school

In explaining the amount of contact or lack of contact between the home and the school it is difficult to distinguish apathy on the part of the parent from lack of encouragement (which can be manifested in various subtle ways) on the part of the school. In the following section we merely describe how much communication there was between parents and teachers in the E.P.A. project schools and do not attempt to attribute failures in communication to either cause.

Table C.13
Parents' views on the functions of parents and of schools

Note: Figures for all four project areas have been grouped together

Function	Percentage thinking function is:					
	School's job %	Parents' job %	Job of both %	Don't know or no reply %	Total %	(N)
Teach children the difference between right and wrong	4	45	51	0	100	(771)
Teach children to talk properly	13	29	57	1	100	(771)
Help children to get to know other children	26	22	47	5	100	(771)
Teach children to keep off the streets and out of mischief	4	65	30	1	100	(771)
Educate children so that they can get a good job	59	6	34	1	100	(771)
Teach children a lot of interesting and useful things	39	11	49	1	100	(771)
Teach children how to behave in public	4	60	35	1	100	(771)
Teach children good manners	2	65	32	1	100	(771)

Table C.14
Helping children at home, by project area

Percentage of families in various categories

	London %	Birmingham %	Liverpool %	West Riding %
Child shows parent what he has been doing	86	77	86	93
Child talks about his work	82	76	84	89
Parent says he/she knows what child is doing at school at the moment	53	25	58	52
Parent helps child if he finds difficulty with his work	63	38	61	62
Child has had reading books bought for him in the past 12 months	69	47	62	83
Child belongs to public library	58	46	28	45
Parent helps child to choose books	31	10	23	29
Total no. of families	(204)	(181)	(191)	(195)

A number of the questions in the survey on parent-school contacts were taken from the national survey among parents of primary school children conducted in 1964 by the Government Social Survey for the Central Advisory Council for Education.[1] This survey achieved 95 per cent coverage of a random sample of over three thousand parents of primary school children in England, and so gives a national standard against which parents' contacts with the E.P.A. project schools can be compared. A little caution is necessary however, for the national survey took place five years before the E.P.A. survey. During this period there may well have been a general trend towards improving arrangements for parents to visit the schools, especially in view of the publication of the Plowden Report in 1967. Thus the contrast between the E.P.A. project schools and the average primary school in 1969 may possibly have been greater than is suggested by a comparison with the results of the 1964 survey. The national survey also differed from the E.P.A. survey in that it was confined to the parents of children in the top infants, bottom juniors, and fourth year juniors. However the differences between parents in the E.P.A. project areas and in the national sample in general could still be observed when we looked only at the parents of E.P.A. children in the same age groups as those in the national sample.

The following description covers the contacts which had taken place between parents and staff during the years immediately preceding the start of the E.P.A. Project. One of the main aims of the project was to foster such contacts, and if a similar survey had been conducted three years later it no doubt would have shown a very different picture.

In many of the aspects of parent-school contacts that were examined there were considerable variations between project areas. For instance, in Table C.15 we see that while only 18 per cent of parents in the London project schools had had no talk with the head when their child first began to attend his present school, 58 per cent of parents in Birmingham had not had a talk. In both Birmingham and the West Riding the proportion

[1] *Children and their Primary Schools: A Report of the Central Advisory Council for Education, Vol. 2, Research and Surveys.* H.M.S.O., 1967, Appendices 3–7.

of parents having such a talk was smaller than in the national survey, while in Liverpool it was about the same and in London considerably greater. Of those who had talked with the head, the majority in all four areas had seen him on their own rather than in the company of other parents. In Birmingham, West Indian parents were less likely to have had a talk with the head than parents of U.K. or Eire origin, though the difference did not reach statistical significance, and although in London as many West Indian as U.K. or Eire parents had seen the head, rather fewer of them had talked with him on their own. Three-quarters of the Asian parents in Birmingham had not seen the head at all when their child first started at his present school, and the difference between them and the U.K. and Eire parents was highly significant statistically.

Table C.15

Whether parents had a talk with the head when child first went to present school, by project area and country of origin, compared with replies to the same question in the 1964 national survey

	No talk with head %	Talk with head on own %	Talk with head with other parents %	No information %	Total %	(N)
All London E.P.A. families	*18*	*59*	*21*	*3*	*100*	*(204)*
U.K. and Eire	17	61	19	3	100	(144)
West Indies	19	51	28	2	100	(47)
All Birmingham E.P.A. families	*58*	*28*	*8*	*6*	*100*	*(181)*
U.K. and Eire	47	42	7	4	100	(72)
West Indies	56	25	8	10	100	(48)
India and Pakistan	77	10	8	6	100	(52)
All Liverpool E.P.A. families	*35*	*51*	*10*	*4*	*100*	*(191)*
All West Riding E.P.A. families	*45*	*32*	*21*	*3*	*100*	*(195)*
*National survey**	*37*	*48*	*14*	*1*	*100*	*(3,092)*

* Source: *Children and their Primary Schools, Vol. 2.* Appendix 3, Table 48 and paragraph 3.16.

With the exception of London, as Table C.16 shows, rather more parents in the project schools than in the national survey had had no talk at all with either the head or their child's classteacher over the whole time he had been at his current school, while the percentage of parents who had had four or more talks was rather smaller. Obviously this variable depends to some extent on the length of time the child had been at the school, but when we compared the national sample with the parents of the seven, eight and eleven year olds in the national survey, the only non-negligible change was in the figures for Birmingham, in which older children were over-represented. The effect was to substantially reduce the difference between the West Indian and the U.K. and Eire group there, and to increase the difference between the latter and the national sample. However the West Indian parents in both London and Birmingham still appeared to have less contact with the schools than the parents of U.K. or Eire origin, and the Asians had substantially less than either group.

Table C.16

Number of talks parents had had with head or classteacher, by project
area and country of origin, compared with replies to the same question
in the 1964 national survey

	Number of talks						
	0	1	2 or 3	4 or more	No information	Total	
	%	%	%	%	%	%	(N)
All London E.P.A. families	9	12	31	48	0	100	(204)
U.K. and Eire	7	10	30	54	0	100	(144)
West Indies	13	21	36	30	0	100	(47)
All Birmingham E.P.A. families	29	17	22	32	1	100	(181)
U.K. and Eire	11	22	22	44	0	100	(72)
West Indies	17	15	31	35	2	100	(48)
India and Pakistan	63	12	15	10	0	100	(52)
All Liverpool E.P.A. families	16	14	36	33	1	100	(191)
All West Riding E.P.A. families	13	16	32	38	1	100	(195)
*National survey**	8	13	33	45	0	100	(3,092)

* Source: *Children and their Primary Schools, Vol. 2,* Appendix 3, Table 49.

In the report of the national survey the question on which Table C.16
is based was interpreted as referring to both parents, though it was addressed
only to the person interviewed who almost always was the mother. A
separate question (Table C.17) showed that on average 50 per cent of
fathers had never visited their child's school as compared with 40 per cent
in the national survey. It seems as though West Indian and Asian fathers
were equally likely to visit the school as fathers of U.K. or Eire origin. It
is the traditional role of the father in Indian and Pakistani families to deal
with outsiders, and it seems as though it is the mothers, who often do not
speak English, who particularly need to be encouraged to come into the
school.

Table C.18 shows the proportion of parents attending various special
activities at their child's school. We cannot distinguish the parents who did
not attend at a particular occasion, although invited, from those who had
not attended because such an occasion had never been arranged, for it was
clear from the replies that if parents had not attended they sometimes
forgot—or perhaps had never been aware—that it had taken place. The
number of E.P.A. families attending on these occasions was generally as
great if not greater than the number attending in the national survey.
However, with the exception of parent-teacher association meetings, rather
fewer West Indian than U.K. or Eire parents attended, and the proportion
of Asian families attending was much smaller.

In the National Survey half of the parents said that they had visited their
child's school without being asked.[1] The corresponding proportion among
U.K. and Eire parents varied between 37 per cent in the West Riding and
60 per cent in London. West Indian parents and more especially Asian
parents were considerably less likely to go up to the school on their own
initiative.

---

[1] *Children and their Primary Schools, Vol. 2,* Appendix 3, paragraph 3.29.

Table C.17

Whether husband had visited child's present school or talked to head, by project area and country of origin, compared with replies to the same question in the 1964 national survey

	Husband visited school and talked to head %	Husband visited school but not talked to head %	Husband had not visited school %	No husband or no informa- tion %	Total %	(N)
All London E.P.A. families	24	18	51	7	100	(204)
U.K. and Eire	24	17	52	6	100	(144)
West Indies	23	19	49	8	100	(47)
All Birmingham E.P.A. families	17	16	51	16	100	(181)
U.K. and Eire	11	15	50	24	100	(72)
West Indies	21	15	48	17	100	(48)
India and Pakistan	21	17	58	4	100	(52)
All Liverpool E.P.A. families	13	9	64	14	100	(191)
All West Riding E.P.A. families	29	23	40	8	100	(195)
*National survey**	30	25	40	5	100	(3,092)

* Source: *Children and their Primary Schools, Vol. 2,* Appendix 3, Table 21.

The extent of non-communication between the home and the school is shown by the fact that only 57 per cent to 74 per cent of parents of U.K. and Eire origin in the different project areas could give the name of their child's classteacher correctly, although all but 10 or 15 per cent knew the head's name (see Table C.19). Rather fewer of the West Indians could give either name—less than half gave the classteacher's name correctly—while only 23 per cent of the Asian mothers knew the head's name and a mere 8 per cent the classteacher's.

The report of the national survey shows in general that the lower a parent's social class, the less his contact with the school.[1] As the parents of children in the E.P.A. project schools were almost all working class, we would expect on these grounds alone that their contact with the schools would be less than the average nationally. It does not follow, however, that this situation cannot be improved. The differences among the four areas show the scope for improvement, as the London project schools appeared to have achieved much better links with parents than the project schools serving similar populations in Birmingham and Liverpool.

Although on the whole West Indian parents had fewer contacts with the schools than the families of U.K. or Eire origin, the gap between them was on the whole fairly narrow, and on a number of measures the West Indian families in London were in a better position than U.K. or Eire families in other areas. The Asian families however posed a real problem, as their contact with their children's teachers appeared minimal. This was

---

[1] *Children and their Primary Schools, Vol. 2,* Appendix 3, paragraphs 3.13 to 3.24.

Table C.18

Parents' attendance at various school activities, by project area and country of origin, compared with the corresponding percentages in the 1964 national survey

| | London E.P.A. | | | Birmingham E.P.A. | | | | Liverpool E.P.A. | West Riding E.P.A. | National Survey* |
	All families %	U.K. and Eire %	West Indies %	All families %	U.K. and Eire %	West Indies %	India and Pakistan %	All families %	All families %	%
						% of families in which either parent attended:				
Open days, prize days, sports days, swimming galas, school plays, shows, concerts, school carol and other services, school outings	72	76	60	54	74	67	19	54	78	—†
Parent-teacher association meetings or other activities	24	24	26	7	4	12	4	17	18	13
Jumble sales, bazaars, social evenings to raise money for the school	45	51	28	46	71	29	27	51	74	49
Medical or dental examinations	81	87	68	68	81	79	40	77	65	72
Total no. of families	(204)	(144)	(47)	(181)	(72)	(48)	(52)	(191)	(195)	(3,092)

* Source: *Children and their Primary Schools, Vol. 2.* Appendix 3. Table 53.

† Table 53 gives separate figures for each of these activities, whereas we amalgamated them for the purposes of analysis; thus no direct comparison is possible.

Table C.19

Whether parent knows the name of selected child's headteacher or classteacher,
by project area and country of origin

	% giving headteacher's name correctly	% giving classteacher's name correctly	Total no. of families
All London parents	84	62	(204)
U.K. and Eire	88	71	(144)
West Indies	74	40	(47)
All Birmingham parents	63	44	(181)
U.K. and Eire	86	74	(72)
West Indies	77	44	(48)
India and Pakistan	23	8	(52)
All Liverpool parents	86	57	(191)
All West Riding parents	88	74	(195)

due probably to a combination of factors. In English families it is usually the mother who deals with the school, partly by tradition and partly because she is more likely to be free during school hours. Asian women however are often totally unaccustomed to dealing with strangers, especially male ones, and in addition they are very often unable to speak English. A number of schools are now attempting to overcome this problem by encouraging Asian women to attend English classes at the school.

The national survey found that despite their lesser contact, working class parents were slightly less critical than middle class parents of arrangements for seeing the head or classteacher. We also found that the large majority of E.P.A. parents of U.K. or Eire origin were satisfied with the various aspects of parent-school contact specified in Table C.20. There were however differences among the areas: parents in the West Riding tended to be more satisfied than parents in the national survey, parents in Birmingham and Liverpool tended to be less satisfied, and parents in London were more satisfied in some respects but less in others. These differences related broadly to the actual extent of contacts between parents and teachers in the four areas, for it will be remembered that these tended to be rather better in London and the West Riding than in Liverpool or Birmingham. West Indian parents in both London and Birmingham had, if anything, more favourable attitudes towards visiting the school, perhaps because their expectations of how they should be received by the school were not as high, but too many of the Asian families felt unable to express an opinion for any comparison to be possible with them.

Children's problems at school and parents' criticisms of the project schools

We have already quoted the finding of the national survey that the lower a parent's social class, the less likely he is to criticise his child's school. The social distance which parents may feel between themselves and teachers may inhibit criticism, and their standards of comparison are probably not as high. Even so, Table C.21 shows that a substantial minority of the E.P.A. parents felt that their child was getting an education worse than most children in Britain, and very few indeed thought that the education they were getting was better. In Birmingham more than twice as many parents

Table C.20

Attitudes of mothers of families of U.K. and Eire origin towards visiting the school, by project area, compared with the attitudes of mothers in the 1964 national survey

Note: The response indicating an unfavourable attitude towards visiting the school is given in brackets after each statement.

	% of interviewees giving the unfavourable response:				
	London %	Birmingham %	Liverpool %	West Riding %	National survey* %
It is very easy to see the teachers whenever you want to (disagree)	8	13	5	3	9
I would feel that I was interfering if I went to the school uninvited (agree)	24	25	26	21	25†
If you go up to the school they only tell you what you know already (agree)	31	32	24	18	20†
The teachers seem very pleased when parents go along to see them (disagree)	10	7	8	2	7
Teachers have enough to do already without having to talk to parents (agree)	28	44	42	28	29
Some teachers seem to have favourites among the parents (agree)	29	18	28	27	19
The teachers definitely seem interested in what *you* think about your child's education (disagree)	16	18	9	6	—‡
I feel that the teachers would like to keep parents out of the school (agree)	13	21	15	6	11
Total no. of respondents	(144)	(72)	(170)	(194)	(3,092)

* Source: *Children and their Primary Schools, Vol. 2,* Appendix 3, paragraphs 3.25 to 3.30.

† Approximate figures only.

‡ This figure is not reported in Vol. 2 of *Children and their Primary Schools.*

of U.K. or Eire origin were dissatisfied than in the other areas, and it will be remembered from Section A that the attainment of children attending the Birmingham project schools was considerably lower than that of children in the project schools elsewhere. Understandably, a number of immigrant parents said they were unable to make a judgment of this kind, though those who did have an opinion were less dissatisfied than the U.K. or Eire parents, and Asian parents appeared to be particularly content.

When those who had said their child's education was worse were asked to specify their dissatisfactions, the most common complaint both among U.K. and Eire and among West Indian parents was of overcrowding and understaffing, including complaints about high teacher turnover and the youth or inexperience of the staff. The survey of teachers reported in Section B showed that in London and Birmingham at least these complaints were amply justified. The second most frequent criticisms were of the teaching

Table C.21

*Whether parents felt their child was getting an education as good as,
better, or worse than most children of the same age in Britain, by project
area and country of origin*

	Better %	As good as %	Worse %	Don't know or no informa- tion %	Total %	(N)
All London parents	4	75	10	11	*100*	*(204)*
U.K. and Eire	3	77	12	8	100	(144)
West Indies	6	72	2	19	100	(47)
All Birmingham parents	8	57	19	16	*100*	*(181)*
U.K. and Eire	4	59	30	6	100	(69)
West Indies	2	67	15	17	100	(48)
India and Pakistan	19	52	6	23	100	(52)
All Liverpool parents	3	75	14	8	*100*	*(191)*
All West Riding parents	4	74	11	10	*100*	*(195)*

methods, and in particular what the parents saw as a lack of formal
instruction in the three "Rs". Next in order of frequency were criticisms
of the area or type of pupils at the school, including the presence of
immigrant children, and complaints about the school buildings and facilities.
Finally, a few parents said that discipline in the schools was poor.

A later question asked all parents what changes they would like to see
in primary schools, and answers to this, given in Table C.22, also put
overcrowding and staffing as first priority. Improvements to buildings or
amenities were equal second with better discipline and more respect for
teachers, and changes in teaching methods appeared only fourth on the
list. As far as this point the priorities of the U.K. and Eire parents
were shared by the West Indians, but 5 per cent of U.K. and Eire parents
also said they would like more information about the school or their child's
progress, and 4 per cent a remedy to the problems they felt were caused
by having immigrant children in the classes. Very few of the Asian parents
were able to suggest any improvements. Differences between the replies of
parents in the different areas reflected the particular problems in some;
thus a reduction in overcrowding and improvement in staffing was mentioned
more frequently in the inner city areas than in the West Riding, and in
Birmingham a much larger proportion of parents than in the other areas
complained of the standard of buildings and amenities and said they were
worried by the numbers of immigrant children.

When asked to compare their child's education with their own (Table
C.23), the majority of parents of U.K. and Eire origin in each area said it was
better, but a significant minority, particularly in Birmingham, felt it was
worse. Many immigrant parents felt that no comparison was possible,
which was clearly so for the Asian mothers who had not been to school at
all, but interestingly a higher proportion of West Indians than of parents
from the British Isles said their child's education was worse than their own.

Table C.22

Changes that parents would like to see in primary schools, by country of origin

Note: Percentages do not total to 100 because some parents did not mention any change and some mentioned more than one.

	All E.P.A. parents %	U.K. and Eire %	West Indies %	India and Pakistan %
Reduction in overcrowding or improvements in staffing	16	18	8	0
Improvements to buildings and amenities	8	10	5	0
More discipline and respect for teachers	8	9	4	2
More formal teaching methods; more hard work	6	6	5	2
More information about school or child's progress	4	5	0	0
Something done about immigrant children	3	4	0	0
Miscellaneous	12	14	18	6
Total no. of parents	(771)	(578)	(95)	(52)

Table C.23

Whether parents thought their child's education was as good as, better, or worse than the education they had at the same age, by project area and country of origin

	Better %	As good as %	Worse %	No information or no comparison possible %	Total %	(N)
All London parents	*51*	*18*	*21*	*10*	*100*	*(204)*
U.K. and Eire	56	18	19	8	100	(144)
West Indies	43	19	21	17	100	(47)
All Birmingham parents	*42*	*12*	*20*	*26*	*100*	*(181)*
U.K. and Eire	55	13	25	7	100	(69)
West Indies	17	21	33	29	100	(48)
India and Pakistan	46	4	6	44	100	(52)
All Liverpool parents	*65*	*16*	*12*	*7*	*100*	*(191)*
All West Riding parents	*61*	*16*	*15*	*8*	*100*	*(195)*

This is consistent with the finding reported in Table C.10 that West Indian parents had on average left school later than parents from the U.K. or Eire.

Table C.24 shows that according to their parents nearly half of the selected children of U.K. or Eire origin had had some kind of problem or difficulty at some time while they had been at school, though the proportion was rather smaller in the West Riding. The largest category of problems concerned the child's relationship with other children, and involved

Table C.24

Children's problems at school and parents' worries about child's progress, by project area and country of origin

Percentage of families in various categories

	London			Birmingham				Liverpool	West Riding
	All families %	U.K. and Eire %	West Indies %	All families %	U.K. and Eire %	West Indies %	India and Pakistan %	All families %	All families %
Child has had some problems at some time while he has been at school	42	43	36	32	46	29	19	45	29
Parent had some worries about the methods of teaching at child's school or the way in which he was getting on in his work	31	33	23	23	26	31	13	18	24
Total number of families	(204)	(144)	(47)	(181)	(69)	(48)	(52)	(191)	(195)

bullying, roughness, teasing and so on—14 per cent of parents complained of this. Next came general anxiety and reluctance to go to school (12 per cent), problems concerning the child's relationship with his classteacher (8 per cent), and domestic problems, illness or specific disabilities (7 per cent). Only 4 per cent of parents said the schoolwork was too difficult.

West Indian parents were less likely to admit the existence of problems, but it is significant that among the problems they specified, relationships with other children were by far the most common—16 per cent mentioned this, as against 6 per cent who mentioned relationships with the classteacher, 5 per cent domestic problems, illness or disabilities, and 4 per cent each general anxiety or reluctance to go and the difficulty of the work. Only 19 per cent of Asian parents said their child had ever had any problem, not enough to allow a breakdown into categories.

Table C.24 also shows that between 18 per cent and 31 per cent of parents in each area said they were currently concerned about the methods of teaching at their child's school or the way in which he was getting on with his work, and in Birmingham a slightly higher proportion of West Indians than of U.K. or Eire parents expressed such worries. West Indian parents have often experienced rather formal teaching methods at school themselves and may find the informal atmosphere of an English primary school disconcerting.

Once more, only a few Asians expressed concern about this matter. Interviewers in social survey work often feel that Asian families are reluctant to admit any problems to an outsider, even though such problems may exist. The manifest difficulties of the Asian children as revealed by the tests of vocabulary and reading[1] show that we would be unwise to take the responses of the Asian families interviewed at face value.

Summary

Despite certain limitations, the survey of parents still yielded a mass of information of a descriptive rather than a hypothesis-testing nature. It showed substantial differences in the stability of the populations in the different project areas and gross inadequacies in the provision of places in nursery schools and playgroups. Though many parents had had only a minimal education they were nevertheless often quite ambitious for their children, but tended to believe that it was the school's function rather than their own to see that they were able to get a good job. Their contacts with the school were rather less than for the average primary school parent, and this was particularly a problem with the Asian families. Finally, a significant minority were dissatisfied with the education their children were receiving, and their complaints reflected the real problems which we knew to exist in the project schools.

---

[1] See Section A.

Appendix to Section C

Questionnaire used in the Survey of Parents

PARENTAL SURVEY

Interviewers' Introduction

We are engaged in a project aimed at improving primary school education, i.e. education for children up to the age of eleven, and we think that it is very important to find out what parents themselves feel about the schools which their children are attending, and whether they, as parents, think that any changes should be made. We are also interested to know what young children are like out of school.

We selected every tenth name on the school register of ....
—your name happened to be chosen, and we hope that you will help. (The school staff have had nothing to do with selecting the parents to be interviewed and will not see the answers.)

All the information you give us will be treated as strictly confidential and no information about individuals will be passed on to anyone outside the research team. Because many fathers would find it difficult to spare time to be interviewed except late in the evenings, we are generally asking mothers to speak for both parents.

Once the information has been collected, it will be combined with information obtained from large numbers of other parents, both in other schools in .... and from other parts of the country. No names will be shown in the results. There is no compulsion to take part in the survey, but its value does depend on the co-operation of the parents we approach, so we hope that you will help by answering a few questions.

If there is any further information you require which the interviewer is unable to supply please get in touch with:—

[Name and address of local research officer]

APPENDIX TO SECTION C

Parental Survey for E.P.A. Project: Questionnaire

(i) Serial number:

School .... (a)

Child .... (b)

(ii) Interviewer's name ....

(iii) Date of interview ....

(iv) Time of starting interview:

Before 11 a.m.	1
11 a.m. up to just before 1 p.m.	2
1 p.m. up to just before 3 p.m.	3
3 p.m. up to just before 5 p.m.	4
5 p.m. up to just before 7 p.m.	5
7 p.m. or after	6

(v) Time interview took:

Less than $\frac{3}{4}$ of an hour	1
$\frac{3}{4}$ but less than 1 hour	2
1 hour but less than $1\frac{1}{4}$ hours	3
$1\frac{1}{4}$ hours but less than $1\frac{1}{2}$ hours	4
$1\frac{1}{2}$ hours but less than 2 hours	5
2 hours or longer	6

(vi) Whether anyone other than informant present during interview:

(Do not count adults or children who were present for less than 5 minutes)

No, only informant present	1
Selected child present	2
Child's father present	3
Other children present, relatives or not	4
Other adults present, relatives or not	5

(vii) Relationship of person interviewed to selected child:

Child's natural mother	1
Foster or adopted mother	2
Other (specify)	

(viii) Age of child .... years.

(ix) Position in family ....

1. I would like to ask you first about the schools .... has been to so far. Did he/she go to a nursery school, nursery class, or organised play group?

   (Code as 'No....3' if attended nursery for less than 1 month in total. Probe if necessary)

Yes, in this country	1
Yes, abroad only	2
No	3
Don't know	4

2. How old was he/she when he/she first started to go to school in the morning *and* afternoons?

   (Include nursery school or class if attended in the mornings and afternoons)

Under $3\frac{1}{2}$ years old	1
$3\frac{1}{2}$ years but less than 4	2
4 years but less than $4\frac{1}{2}$	3
$4\frac{1}{2}$ years but less than 5	4
5 years but less than $5\frac{1}{2}$	5
$5\frac{1}{2}$ years but less than 6	6
6 years or older	7
Don't know	8

3. Was that a good age for him/her to start or would you have liked him/her to have started earlier or later?
   (This refers to starting in the mornings <u>and</u> afternoons)

Good age to start	1
Earlier start preferred	2
Later start preferred	3
Don't know/not sure	4

   (a) If earlier/later start preferred (2 or 3): At what age would you have liked .... to have started?
   (This refers to mornings <u>and</u> afternoons at school)

Under 3½ years old	1
3½ years but less than 4	2
4 years but less than 4½	3
4½ years but less than 5	4
5 years but less than 5½	5
5½ years but less than 6	6
6 years or older	7
Don't know	8

   (b) Why would you have preferred this age?
   (Prompt only if necessary)
   If later start preferred:

Too young when started	1
Not ready to learn	2
Mother prefers child at home	3
Not happy to be separated	4
Others, specify:	

   If earlier start preferred:

To get child out of house	1
To give mother more free time	2
Child sufficiently grown up	3
Child ready to learn	4
Wanted to be with brothers/sisters	5
Wanted to be with other children	6
Child bored at home	7
Mother too busy	8
Others, specify:	

4. (a) When .... first went to infants school did he/she attend school in the mornings *and* afternoons, or only in the mornings *or* afternoons?

Attended morning *and* afternoons immediately	1
Attended mornings only at first	2
Attended afternoons only at first	3
Don't know/can't remember	4

   (b) Was this completely satisfactory?

Yes	1
No	2
Don't know	3

   (c) If number (2), would you have preferred:

Mornings *and* afternoons	4
Mornings *only*	5
Afternoons *only*	6

5. (a) Has .... been to any other schools?

         Yes 1
         No 2
         Don't know 3

    (b) If yes (1) specify:
         Nursery school or playgroup 1
         Feeding infant school 2
         Other area 3
         Other school same area 4

    (c) If (4) i.e. moved school within area, why did ....
    leave? (open-ended)

6. How long has .... been at *(present school)*?

         One term or less 1
         Over 1 term, up to and exactly 1 school year 2
         Over 1 school year, up to and exactly 2 school years 3
         Over 2 school years, up to and exactly 3 school years 4
         Over 3 school years 5
         Don't know 6

7. Have any other members of your family been to *(present school)*?
    (Prompt as necessary)

         No, not as far as parent knows 1
         Yes, brothers, sisters of selected child (include steps, etc.) 2
         Yes, father, mother 3
         Yes, other relatives, e.g. uncle, aunt, cousin 4

8. (a) Some children find it difficult to settle in at school. When ....
    first started school, was he/she happy?

         Yes 1
         No 2

    (b) If yes (1) what do you think particularly helped him/her to settle in?
         Nice teacher 1
         Nice school 2
         Good mixer 3
         Friends at the school 4
         Elder brother or sister already there 5
         Well prepared by mother.. 6
         Others, specify:

    (c) If no (2) why do you think .... was unhappy?
         Doesn't like teacher 1
         Dislikes discipline 2
         Different class from brothers, sisters or friends 3
         Worried about being away from mother 4
         Domestic problems 5
         Not a good mixer 6
         Doesn't speak English 7
         Don't know 8
         Others, specify:

9. Has .... been quite happy in school *this* term or has he/she been worried or disturbed at all?

Child has been quite happy 1
Child worried or disturbed 2
Don't know/can't say 3

(a) If child has been worried or disturbed (2), in what way has he/she been worried or disturbed?

Change of class 1
Domestic problems 2
Teacher problems 3
Difficulty with other children 4
Lonely... 5
Child different standard from rest of class................................... 6
Don't know 7
Others, specify:

10. If .... asked you about what school would be like before he/she started, what did you tell him/her?
(Prompt only if necessary)

Child didn't ask... 1
Nothing don't know 2
Playing all day 3
Learning to read, write and count 4
Meeting other children.. 5
Pleasant experience 6
Unpleasant experience 7
Have to behave and be quiet 8
Joining brothers and sisters.. 9
Child knew all about school from brothers and sisters anyway 10
Others, specify:

11. What parts of school life were completely new to him when he first started?
(Ring all those that apply: prompt only if necessary)

Reading (books) 1
Writing 2
Sums/numbers 3
Playing with lots of other children 4
Being away from mother 5
Type of school meals 6
Discipline/being confined 7
Others, specify:

12. Were you able to help him/her to prepare for school before he/she started? Specify type of help:
    (Prompt only if necessary)

Teaching him/her to read	1
Teaching him/her to write	2
Teaching him/her numbers	3
Telling stories, nursery rhymes, etc.	4
Making things	5
Drawing pictures for him/her	6
Providing books	7
Providing educational toys, games, puzzles, etc.	8
Nothing	9
Don't know	10

13. Did your husband or any older children help him/her to prepare for school before he/she started?

Husband	1
Older related children	2
Older non-related children	3
No-one	4

(a) What type of help?
    (Prompt only if necessary)

Teaching him/her to read	1
Teaching him/her to write	2
Teaching him/her numbers	3
Telling stories, nursery rhymes, etc.	4
Making things	5
Drawing pictures for him/her	6
Providing books	7
Providing educational toys, games, puzzles, etc.	8

14. How important do you think it is for children to speak well?

Very important	1
Quite important	2
Not very important	3
Quite unimportant	4
Very unimportant	5
Question not understood	6

15. What differences do you think being able to speak well makes to a child?
    (Ring all that apply: prompt if necessary)

Increases confidence, helps get on with people, makes better mixer	1
Helps person get a good job	2
Helps immigrant's assimilation	3
Poor speech is a reflection on a child's parents	4
Helps children to read/spell/communicate	5
No difference, it is not important	6
May make children appear snobbish	7
Respondent confuses speaking well with politeness	8
Don't know	9

16. Do you try to help .... to speak well?

Yes	1
No	2
Don't know	3

If yes (1)
(a) What do you correct?
     (Ring all those that apply: prompt if necessary)
                  Bad grammar.. 1
                  Bad pronunciation/local accent 2
                  Slang/swearing/shouting 3
                  Baby talk 4
                  Bad manners (please and thank you) 5
                  Don't know 6
                  Others, specify:

(b) How do you correct it?
     (Ring all those that apply: prompt if necessary)
                  Making them repeat things 1
                  Non-English-speaking mother.. 2
                  By example.. 3
                  Reprimand/telling off 4
                  Telling them *why* it is wrong 5
                  Don't know 6
                  Others, specify:

17. (a) Does .... ever ask you the meaning of words?
                  Yes 1
                  No 2
                  Don't know 3

     (b) If yes (1), how would you explain the meaning of the word?
          (Code no more than two. Prompt only if necessary)
                  Can't/don't know 1
                  Non-English-speaking mother.. 2
                  Use in context 3
                  Put into simple terms 4
                  Refer to dictionary 5
                  Tell child to ask father 6
                  Tell child to ask brother, sister or friend 7
                  Tell child to ask teacher 8

18. (a) Do you have a dictionary in the house?
                  Yes 1
                  No 2
                  Don't know 3

     (b) If yes (1), how often is it used?
                  Often 1
                  Sometimes 2
                  Never 3

19. Could you tell me whose class .... is in?
     (Ring 1 or 2)
                  Yes 1
                  No 2
     Code later $\begin{cases}\text{Correct} \\ \text{Incorrect}\end{cases}$ 3
                                                                                                    4

20. Do you know the headmaster's/headmistress's name?
    (Ring 1 or 2)

Yes	1
No	2
Code later $\left\{ \begin{array}{l} \text{Correct ....} \\ \text{Incorrect...} \end{array} \right.$	3
	4

21. Can we talk now about the contacts parents have with the teachers at ....'s present school? Did you have a talk with the head when .... first went to *(present school)*?
    (Code 1 if talked to head just before child started, if talked to deputy or assistant head, or if parent knew head personally at that time)

Yes	1
No	2
Don't know/can't remember	3

    (a) If yes (1): Apart perhaps from .... being there, did the head talk to you on your own or with other parents?

Talked to mother and/or father on own (or knows head personally)	1
Talked to mother/father with other parents	2
Don't know/can't remember	3

22. *If husband and wife in household*
    Has your husband been able to go to ....'s school at all?

No husband/wife	1
Yes	2
No	3
Don't know/can't remember	4

    (a) If yes (2), has he talked with the head at all?

Yes	1
No	2
Don't know	3

23. About how often have you had a talk about .... with the head, or with ....'s classteacher since he/she started there?

No talk with head or teacher	1
One talk with head or teacher	2
Two talks with head or teacher	3
Three talks with head or teacher..	4
Four talks with head or teacher	5
Four to six talks with head or teacher[1]	6
More than six talks with head or teacher	7

    (a) *If had a talk with head or classteacher* (2 to 7)
        Have you ever been to see the head *without* him/her asking?

Yes	1
No	2
Don't know/can't remember	3

[1] Sic.

(b) We would like to know what sort of things parents want to be able to see the teachers about. Would you mind telling me what sort of things you have been to see the head or ....'s teacher about?
(Include all visits, whether initiated by the head or parent)

	Has	Might
No visit made	1	1
Child's progress educationally, teaching methods used	2	2
To notify school of illness, holiday, other absence from school	3	3
Behavioural problems of informant's child, e.g. nervousness, worry, bad behaviour...	4	4
To discuss or look for lost items of clothing and other property	5	5

Others, specify:

(c) If no visit has been made (1) ask what sort of thing do you think you *might* visit the school about, and code in above.

24. I am going to read out a list of things which some schools provide for parents.
(a) I would like you to tell me whether *(present school)* has had any of these since .... started there: *prompt list below and record in* (a)
(b) *For each item coded 1 in* (a) *ask:* Have you (or your husband) been able to go to any of these? *Record in* (b).

PROMPT LIST

	(a) Whether school has this			(b) Whether attended	
	Yes	No	Don't know	Mother and/or father attended	Neither attended or don't know
(i) Open days (including open evenings)					
(ii) Prize days					
(iii) Sports days, swimming galas					
(iv) School plays, shows, concerts, school carol and other services					
(v) Parent-teacher association meetings or other activities					
(vi) School outings					
(vii) Jumble sales, bazaars, social evenings to raise money for school					
(viii) Medical or dental examinations......					

25. Are there any (other) things which you have been to at *(present school)* which I haven't mentioned?
Specify:

26. I am going to read out some things that parents have said about going to their children's schools. I would like you to tell me whether you feel the same way or not about *(present school)*.

	Feels the same; agrees	Does not feel this; disagrees	Don't know; neither agrees nor disagrees; no personal experience; can't answer
(i) It's very easy to see the teachers whenever you want to..................			
(ii) I would feel that I was interfering if I went to the school uninvited			
(iii) If you go up to the school they only tell you what you know already......			
(iv) The teachers seem very pleased when parents go along to see them			
(v) I feel that teachers have enough to do already without having to talk to parents			
(vi) Some teachers seem to have favourites among the parents..................			
(vii) The teachers definitely seem interested in what *you* think about your child's education			
(viii) I feel that the teachers would like to keep parents out of the school			

27. Here are some things which some parents have suggested junior schools should do. I would like you to tell me whether you think the school should do them or whether they are the parents' job.
    (*Tick in appropriate column*)

	Parents' job	School's job	Both	Don't know
(i) Teach children the difference between right and wrong..................				
(ii) Teach children to talk properly				
(iii) Help children to get to know other children				
(iv) Teach children to keep off streets and out of mischief				
(v) Educate children so that they can get a good job				
(vi) Teach children a lot of interesting and useful things				
(vii) Teach children how to behave in public......................................				
(viii) Teach children good manners				

28. Are you quite happy with the present arrangements at *(present school)* for seeing the head or classteacher?
    Completely happy with present arrangements, no reservations 1
    Not completely happy with present arrangements 2
    Don't know/can't say 3

    (a) If not completely happy (2): Could you tell me what sort of arrangements you would prefer and also what you think can be done to make it easier for teachers and mothers to get together?
        (*Ring all that apply*)
        Should be able to/easier to see classteacher 1
        Should be able to see head, classteacher *in private* 2
        Should be a parent-teacher association 3
        Should be more meetings in the evenings 4
        Should be someone who would visit you at home 5
        Don't know 6
        Others, specify:

29. (a) Would you be prepared to help out at school?
        Yes 1
        No 2

(b) If yes (1), what sort of things would you be prepared to do?
Collect for charity 1
Show people around on open day 2
Do weekly dinner duties 3
Supervise children in playground 4
Making things for the school 5
Others, specify:

30. Can we talk about the methods of teaching which they use at *(present school)*?
Has the head, or have any of the other teachers talked to you about the methods they use at *(present school)*?
(e.g. about the way they teach different subjects, or what they are trying to do in the school.)
Yes, parent has had a talk alone or in a group of parents 1
Parent has received leaflet, but not had a talk 2
No, no leaflet or talk 3
Don't know/can't remember 4

31. Do you feel quite happy about the methods of teaching used at *(present school)* and the way .... is getting on in his/her work, or is there anything which worries you at all?
Quite happy with methods being used *and* with child's progress 1
Worried about methods and/or child's progress, including worried because does not know how child is getting on.............................. 2
(a) *If worried* (2): What is it that worries you?
(Ring all those that apply)
Feels that child is not up to standard for his/her age, and not being brought on fast enough 1
Not enough individual attention given, particularly to backward, slow pupils, classes too large, teacher not interested in child's progress ... 2
Too much time spent on play or other subjects which parent feels are *not* useful for child's work progress 3
Criticisms of or anxiety about new methods of teaching, e.g. of reading, spelling, arithmetic 4
Does not know how child is getting on. Would like to be told more about, to have reports on, child's progress 5
Fault in child, untidy, won't pay attention, lazy, too talkative/backward 6
Others, specify:

32. (a) If the school were to organise meetings for the parents of ....'s class to hear about teaching methods would either of you go?
Yes 1
No 2

(b) If yes, would both of you go or only you or only your husband?
Both 3
Wife only 4
Husband only 5

(c) What would be the best time for such a meeting at the school to start? Ask for husband/wife as applicable.

	Husband (i)	Wife (ii)
4.00 in the afternoon		
4.30 ,, ,, ,,		
5.00 ,, ,, ,,		
5.30 ,, ,, ,,		
6.00 ,, ,, ,,		
6.30 ,, ,, ,,		
7.00 ,, ,, ,,		
7.30 ,, ,, ,,		
8.00 ,, ,, ,,		
8.30 ,, ,, ,,		
Saturday morning		

(d) If no (2 above), why wouldn't you/your husband go?
(Tick as appropriate)   Husband   Wife
                                                              (i)   (ii)
No time   ....
Not interested ....
Others   ....

33.   (a) At any time while... has been at school has he/she had problems or difficulties of any kind?
                    Yes 1
                    No 2

        (b) If yes, what were they?
             (Ring all that apply)
                    Anxiety (general), reluctant to go 1
                    Didn't like teacher   2
                    Thought teacher didn't like him 3
                    Didn't like other children.. 4
                    Other children didn't like him.. 5
                    Work too hard 6
                    Domestic problems 7
                    Others, specify:

        (c) Do you feel satisfied with the way the school dealt with the problem?
                    Satisfied 1
                    Dissatisfied.. 2
                    Not applicable 3

(d) If dissatisfied (2), specify why?

34. (a) If the school sent out an invitation to you and your husband to have a *private* talk
      with ....'s classteacher would either of you go?
      Yes 1
      No 2

  (b) If yes, would you both go or only you or only your husband?
      Both 3
      Wife only 4
      Husband only 5

35. (a) Do you think that your child is getting an education as good as, better or worse
      than most children of the same age in Britain?
      As good as 1
      Better 2
      Worse 3
      Don't know 4

  (b) If worse (3), specify dissatisfactions:

36. Do you think your child's education is as good as, better or worse than the education
you had at the same age?
      Good as 1
      Better 2
      Worse 3
      Don't know 4
      No comparison possible 5

37. (i) Do you think that there has been much change in primary schools since you were
      there?
      No comparison possible 1
      Yes 2
      No 3

  (ii) If yes (2), specify what sort of difference:
      (Ring all those that apply)
      What they teach 4
      Way they teach 5
      Behaviour 6
      Discipline 7
      Attitudes of teachers.. 8
      Equipment 9
      Others, specify:

(a) Do you think these changes are for the better?

Yes 1

No 2

(b) If no (2), why not? Specify:

(c) What changes would you like to see? Specify:
(Regional suggestions, specific to proposed plan, prompt)

38. (a) Is there anything you would like to know about ....'s
school?

Yes 1

No 2

(b) If yes, specify:

39. How do you think that you could make the teachers' job easier? Specify:

40. How do you think the teachers could make your job easier? Specify:

41. (a) Do you think .... is brighter than you were at
that age?

Yes 1

No 2

(b) What makes you think so? Specify:

42. What would you like your child to do for a living? Specify:

43. What would your child like to do for a living? Specify:

44. (a) Has anyone bought any books for .... in the past 12 months?
                Yes 1
                No 2

    (b) If yes (1), what were they?

45. (a) Is .... in the public library?
                Yes 1
                No 2

    (b) If yes (1), what sort of books does he/she get out? Specify:
                Adventure 1
                Non-fiction (informative)... 2
                Grown up 3
                Childish 4

    (c) If no (2), does he/she get hold of books anywhere else?
        (Ring all those that apply)
                School library 1
                Friends 2
                Buys them 3
                Supply of books in the house 4
                Others, specify:

46. (a) Do you help him/her to choose books?
                Yes 1
                No 2

    (b) Incidentally, what type of books do you like to read? Specify:

47. Are you in the library yourself?
                Yes 1
                No 2

48. (a) Do you find that you have much time for playing card games or dominoes or things like that with ....?
                Yes 1
                No 2

    (b) If yes, how often do you play?

49. (a) Do you encourage .... to read the daily newspaper
    or magazines that you take?

    Yes 1
    No 2
    None regularly taken 3

(b) Incidentally, which ones do you take? Specify:

50. (a) Do you ever find it possible for the whole family to go out on trips to the zoo or
    the seaside or a picnic?

    Yes 1
    No 2

(b) If yes, give examples:

51. (a) Do you or your husband have any hobbies in which the children can take part?

    Yes 1
    No 2

(b) If yes (1), what are they? Specify:

52. What are your *main* hobbies? Specify:

53. I realise from what you have told me that you are very busy, but when you and your
    husband have spare time, do you prefer to spend it:

    Together *away* from the children 1
    Together *with* the children 2
    Husband on his own.. 3
    Wife on her own 4
    Question not applicable 5

54. Do the children help choose T.V. programmes etc., or do you or your husband usually
    decide on your own?

    Children 1
    Mother 2
    Husband.. 3

55. (a) Do you find that .... is able to *help* you much
    around the house (or father in the garden)? For instance, some children might help
    with the washing up or make the beds.

    Yes 1
    No 2

(b)   If yes (1), specify:

56. Have you noticed any changes in .... since he/she started school?
Specify:

57. What changes would you have liked to have seen? Specify:

58. Does .... bring work home?
        Yes 1
        No 2

59. Does .... show you what he/she has been doing?
        Yes 1
        No 2

60. Does .... talk about his/her work?
        Yes 1
        No 2

61. (a) Do you know what he/she is doing at school at the moment?
        Yes 1
        No 2

     (b) If yes (1), what is he/she doing at school at the moment? *(Probe)*

62. At what *age* would you like your child to leave school? Specify:
                                Age .... yrs.

63. How important do you think it is that .... does well
at school?
        Very important indeed 1
        Important 2
        Just a matter of necessity 3
        Not very important 4
        Doesn't matter 5

64. *Boys:* Which would make you more pleased and which would make your husband more pleased?

	Wife	Husband
(a) If .... got into school football team		
(b) If .... was near the top of the class		

(Tick the appropriate box for wife/husband)

Girls: Which would make you more pleased, and which would make your husband more pleased?

	Wife	Husband
(a) If .... were good at household things, knitting, sewing, cooking, etc.		
(b) If .... were near the top of the class		

(Tick the appropriate box for wife/husband)

65. Are there any subjects at school which .... finds particularly difficult? Specify:

66. (a) If .... finds difficulty with his/her work do you try to help with it?
        Yes 1
        No 2

  (b) If no (2), specify whether
        (a) Because never happened.. 3
        (b) Not able to help 4

  (c) If yes (1), give an example of when this happened:

  (d) Was your help successful?
        Yes 5
        No 6

67. What is your husband's job? Specify:

68. (a) Do you work yourself?
        Yes 1
        No 2

(b) If yes (1), what work do you do? Specify:

(c) If no (2), did you work before you were married?
        Yes 1
        No 2

(d) If yes (1), what work did you do? Specify:

69. At what age did your husband leave school? Specify:

        Don't know 1

70. At what age did you leave school? Specify:

        Don't know 1

71. (a) Have you ever been to any evening classes at night school or technical college?
            Yes 1
            No 2

     (b) If yes (1), specify:

72. (a) Has your husband?
            Yes 1
            No 2

     (b) If yes (1), specify:

73. Do you think that most people around here feel the same way about their children's
     education as you do?
            Yes (feel same way) 1
            No (feel differently) 2
            Don't know 3

74. Does .... play with the children around here after school?

     Yes 1
     No 2
     Don't know 3

75. (a) How long have you lived here?

    (b) If less than five years, where did you live before then?

76. Do many of your relatives live near here?

     Yes 1
     No 2
     Don't know 3

77. Do many of your husband's relatives live near here?

     Yes 1
     No 2
     Don't know 3

78. (a) Were you brought up in this area yourself?

     Yes 1
     No 2

    (b) If no (2), where were you brought up? Specify:

79. (a) Was your husband brought up in this area himself?

     Yes 1
     No 2
     Don't know 3

    (b) If no (2), where was he brought up? Specify:

80. Do many of your friends live near here?

     Yes 1
     No 2
     Don't know 3

81. (a) Do you agree with your husband on how to bring up children?

     Yes, agree 1
     No, disagree 2
     Don't know 3

    (b) If no (2), specify any disagreements:

82. Do you try to bring up your children as your mother brought you up?

     Yes 1
     No 2
     Don't know 3

122

INTERVIEWER'S NOTES

State of home:

Co-operativeness/Unco-operativeness:

Obvious domestic problems:

Assessment of respondent's spoken English: 1, 2, 3, 4, 5.

SECTION D

Profiles of the Project Schools

As well as carrying out the three main surveys of pupils, teachers and parents, a considerable amount of information was collected by the local research officers from the project schools' own records. The most striking feature of this data was the tremendous amount of variation among schools even within one area in the degree to which they suffered from different kinds of problems. For this reason we have chosen to present the information not as a set of averaged figures, but as profiles of individual schools. In this way we can show both the wide range there is among schools on each particular measure, and the way in which some schools appear to face an accumulation of problems which probably are causally related to each other.

In order to bring out the differences more vividly we have given the profiles of the London project schools in graphic form. Unfortunately there is not space to present the profiles of the schools in the other three areas in the same way, and these are set out in Table D.1. It is hoped that after studying Figure D(1) the reader will be able to assimilate the information in the table more easily.

The catchment areas of the inner ring E.P.A. schools were subject to large and sudden fluctuations in population as streets of old housing were demolished, new estates built, or immigrant families, possibly with several small children, settled there. These population movements had dramatic effects on the schools: thus in School 5 in London the school roll was 40 per cent greater in 1969 than it was five years previously, while School 6 was only 72 per cent of its 1965 size. Variations as extreme as this occurred in both Birmingham and Liverpool, and even in the West Riding project area, where the population was very stable, slum clearance programmes had considerably reduced the number of pupils at some schools while others had grown rapidly.

The suddenness and size of some of these fluctuations made it very difficult for the schools to adapt to them, and their effect was marked both on the ratio of pupils to teachers and on the degree of physical overcrowding. Although pupil-teacher ratios (including the head and full-time equivalents of part-time teachers) were generally favourable in the London project schools compared with the average for all primary schools in greater London in January 1969[1] they tended to be worse in the schools which had experienced a sudden growth in numbers, and this tendency was also noticeable in the other three areas.

The mean pupil-teacher ratio for all primary schools in England and Wales in January 1969 was 27·7,[2] and although the majority of schools in London and Liverpool had ratios better than this, four of the seven project schools in Birmingham and seven out of ten in the West Riding were worse off than the average primary school.

---

[1] *Statistics of Education 1969, Vol. 1: Schools.* H.M.S.O., 1970, Table 11.

[2] *Ibid.*

Table D.1
Profiles of the project schools in Birmingham, Liverpool and the West Riding

Note: Unless otherwise specified, the figures refer to the position at January 1969.

	Date built	No. on roll	No. on roll as a percentage of no. in January 1965, in January of:				No. of pupils per			Median length of stay of staff	Mean no. of weeks absence per pupil during school year 1968/69	Percentage of pupils			
			1966 %	1967 %	1968 %	1969 %	Teacher*	Classroom†	1,000 square feet‡			Transferring to school during school year 1968/69§ %	Transferring from school during school year 1968/69• %	Immigrants (D.E.S. definition)** %	On free meals list last day of summer term 1969 %
Birmingham project schools:															
1 (infants)	1879	256	112	114	110	108	24	37	27	1 yr.	4·2 weeks	18	21	44	9
2 (junior with infants)	1896	739	106	119	119	118	29	34	26	1 yr. 1 term	3·4 weeks	13	22	43	10
3 (junior with infants)	1876	650	105	108	107	105	32	38	41	2 yrs. 1 term	4·8 weeks	24	20	45	•20
4 (junior with infants)	1958	251	103	100	98	97	28	36	24	5 yrs.	4·4 weeks	32	16	35	18
5 (junior with infants)	1885	532	109	126	116	115	31	33	28	1 term	4·2 weeks	14	25	57	12
6 (junior with infants)	1880	496	95	90	89	86	26	31	23	1 yr. 1 term	5·0 weeks	16	6	45	13
7 (juniors)	1878	327	98	101	106	107	27	27	23	1 term	3·2 weeks	18	17	45	16
Liverpool project schools:															
1 (infants)	1873	114	106	71	62	72	25	16	10	5 yrs. 2 terms	4·4 weeks	18	18	4	16
2 (infants)	1881	152	93	92	82	93	25	22	11	2 yrs.	6·2 weeks	7	31	20	22
3 (infants)	1878	136	99	94	99	63	23	27	16	4 yrs. 1 term	5·1 weeks	6	25	0	37
4 (infants)	1882	228	101	95	87	83	27	25	16	7 yrs. 1 term	4·7 weeks	5	6	0	22
5 (infants)	1875	149	108	110	108	104	28	21	24	3 yrs. 1 term	5·8 weeks	10	24	5	38
6 (junior with infants)	1875	266	97	101	107	102	28	33	11	1 yr. 1 term	5·5 weeks	8	10	0	29
7 (jun. with infants)††	1914	162	86	61	56	45	23	—††	—††	9 yrs. 1 term	6·3 weeks	2	12	0	32
8 (junior with infants)	1873	170	83	74	72	70	26	14	10	16 yrs.	4·2 weeks	16	20	1	21
9 (junior with infants)	1877	235	84	80	86	78	25	17	13	4 yrs.	4·5 weeks	13	32	18	33
10 (junior with infants)	1847	177	98	116	125	132	25	14	9	1 yr. 2 terms	5·9 weeks	8	16	0	28
11 (juniors)	1873	166	94	78	62	55	21	12	10	4 yrs. 1 term	4·6 weeks	14	20	1	38
13 (juniors)	1881	188	100	96	92	82	25	24	11	2 yrs. 2 terms	4·6 weeks	18	28	11	22
14 (juniors)	1878	212	104	100	113	110	29	26	16	1 yr. 1 term	4·0 weeks	2	18	0	40
15 (juniors)	1881	162	93	103	88	71	27	23	16	2 yrs.	3·6 weeks	4	15	0	18
16 (juniors)	1913	180	98	98	93	84	25	20	16	17 yrs. 1 term	3·6 weeks	5	13	1	20
(juniors)	1875	211	104	104	109	106	26	35	24	4 yrs. 1 term	5·5 weeks	12	28	1	34

West Riding project schools:

1 (infants)	1911	115	94	88	87	95	33	23	17	nil	5·5 weeks	10	15	0	27
2 (infants)	1893	127	94	101	93	78	25	25	14	18 yrs. 2 terms	3·8 weeks	5	16	0	19
3 (infants)	1952	198	104	98	106	98	28	16	17	3 yrs.	4·1 weeks	10	6	0	28
4 (infants)	1902	162	96	92	98	123	38	40	31	7 yrs. 2 terms	4·2 weeks	7	4	0	9
5 (junior with infants)	1959	354	106	109	110	106	31	35	24	2 terms	3·3 weeks	5	5	0	21
6 (junior with infants)	1926	299	98	97	97	93	28	30	23	4 yrs. 2 terms	5·1 weeks	3	4	0	13
7 (juniors)	1911	169	101	106	104	105	31	34	21	1 yr. 1 term	3·8 weeks	9	8	0	27
8 (juniors)	1893	151	92	89	80	67	22	22	18	14 yrs. 2 terms	3·0 weeks	1	9	0	16
9 (juniors)	1872	338	102	105	106	106	29	34	28	1 yr. 1 term	2·4 weeks	3	3	0	18
10 (juniors)	1902	213	104	114	116	125	28	30	26	5 yrs. 1 term	2·7 weeks	6	3	0	13

* Including headteachers, and evaluating the service of part-time teachers as a proportion of the full school week.

† Counting purpose-built classrooms only, and thus excluding halls, dining rooms etc. which may be used for teaching.

‡ Based on the total area of the school buildings, including corridors, toilets, etc.

§ Excluding children who were part of the normal entry for that year.

• Excluding those leaving the school at the normal time, having completed the course.

** See page 6

†† The junior and infant departments of an all-age school. In general figures have been extracted for these departments only, but this was not possible for the number of pupils per classroom and per 1,000 square feet.

Figure D(1): Profiles of the London project schools

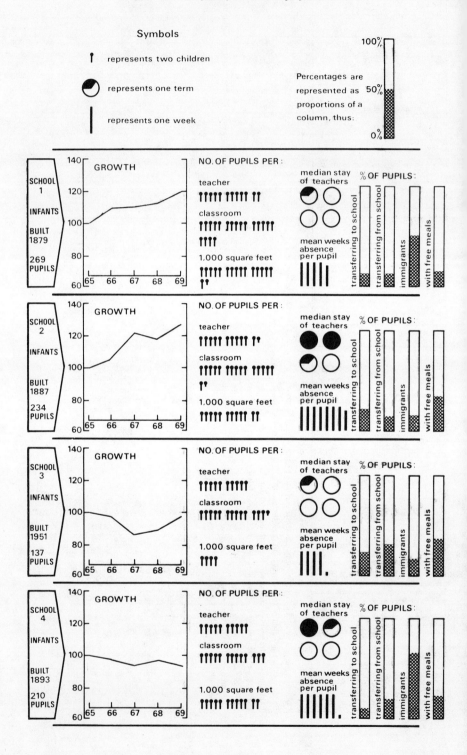

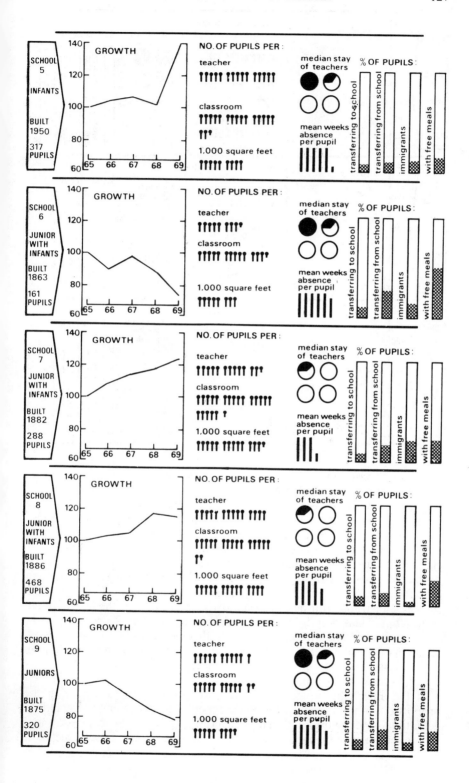

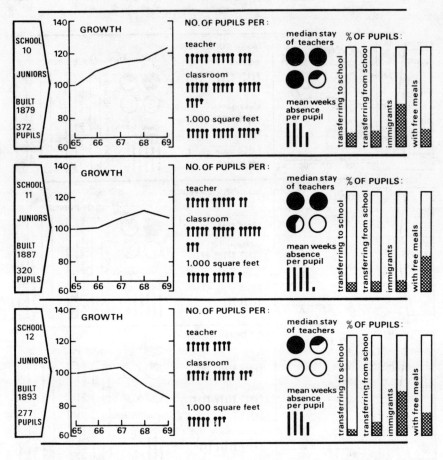

Physical accommodation is even less readily adapted to a sudden growth in numbers than the number of staff. Our two measures of overcrowding—the number of pupils per classroom and per 1,000 square feet[1]—showed a strong relationship with change in pupil numbers, especially when allowance is made for the fact that the more recently built schools appeared to have more spacious standards of accommodation. The number of pupils per classroom varied in London from 25 in a school which was at 83 per cent of its size five years previously to 41 in a school which had grown to 123 per cent of its former numbers. In Liverpool the range was from 35 to 12 per classroom (in a school whose roll had been almost halved), and in the West Riding from 40 per classroom in a school which had grown by 23 per cent to 16 per classroom in one whose numbers had dropped slightly. Pupils per 1,000 square feet varied in general in proportion. In Birmingham the variation on either measure was not quite as apparent, but here most schools were in any case overcrowded by general standards.

In the inner ring project areas there were also wide variations in the proportions of immigrant pupils on the school roll. According to the D.E.S. definition, 4 per cent of children in Liverpool, 24 per cent in London and 46 per cent in Birmingham were immigrants—there were none in the West

---

[1] See Table D.1 for exact definitions.

Riding. In London and Liverpool these children were by no means evenly distributed among the project schools: three of the London schools had no more than one in ten immigrant pupils on their rolls, while four schools had more than four in ten. In Liverpool eight project schools had no immigrant pupils at all while two had almost one in five. In the Birmingham schools the proportions were more constant but high, ranging from 35 per cent to 57 per cent.

As might be expected, pupil turnover presented a serious problem in all the project areas except the West Riding. As a measure of this we took the number of pupils transferring to and from the schools during the course of the school year 1968–69, excluding those entering or leaving at the normal points, and expressed these as percentages of the total number on the roll in January of that year. The results were startling. Ten per cent of the pupils at the London project schools entered the school during the course of the year, and 15 per cent left. In Birmingham the corresponding figures were 18 per cent and 19 per cent, and in Liverpool, 9 per cent and 19 per cent, while in the West Riding schools in contrast pupil turnover was only 5 per cent entering and 6 per cent leaving. Fluctuations between schools were large: 22 per cent of the pupils of School 3 in London transferred to the school during 1968–69 and 31 per cent left, while School 5 had a relatively stable body of pupils. In the worst affected schools the figures represent a considerable degree of disruption to the continuity of the schoolwork.

Absenteeism was also high. Taking the total number of absences as a percentage of the number of possible attendances during 1968–69, we found 11 per cent absenteeism in the West Riding and Birmingham, 13 per cent in Liverpool and 14 per cent in London. These figures may be compared with a count for all I.L.E.A. primary schools, based on a census taken on one day in September 1968, of 8·5 per cent.[1] Again there were variations among schools, but in only five (four of these in the West Riding) was absenteeism as low as the I.L.E.A. average. In ten schools it was greater than 15 per cent, which means a loss of approximately five and a half weeks per pupil during the school year.

We also recorded the number of pupils receiving free meals at the end of the summer term 1969. The count was made shortly after the criterion of eligibility for free meals had changed from one including family size as an entitlement to one based solely on income. The new criterion was applied earlier in some schools than in others, and hence the figures are not wholly reliable as an indicator of the poverty of the families sending children to the schools. However a substantial number of children in every school received free meals, and in more than half of them the number represented over a fifth of those on the school roll.

Finally, we calculated the median[2] length of time for which teachers had stayed in each school. The problem of staff turnover was discussed at some length in the account of the survey of teachers,[3] and the figures taken directly from the school records confirmed the overall picture of a high turnover in London and Birmingham and of stability in the West Riding. No reliable figures were available from the survey of teachers for the Liverpool project schools, but the school records suggested that staff turnover was considerably

---

[1] *I.L.E.A. Research Report No. 2A* (mimeo), January 1972, p. 2.

[2] The median is the point above and below which there is an equal number of cases.

[3] Page 26 ff.

less there than in the other two inner city areas. The records also showed up quite large variations among the schools within each area, which were presumably due to a number of factors, some purely chance, which we could not measure.

Statistical Details of the National Pre-School Experiment

The design of the national pre-school experiment and the conclusions that were drawn from it are described quite fully in the first volume of this series.[1] However precise details of the test scores of the children taking part were omitted from that account, and these are now given in Tables E.1 to E.3.

The differences between treatment and control groups in the experiment in the amount by which their test scores changed during the course of the year were evaluated by the technique of analysis of variance. Very few of the differences proved to be statistically significant, and it was not thought worthwhile to report the details of the analyses here. We also examined the correlation of change in test score with age and time between pre-test and post-test, lest differences between experimental and control groups in these respects should obscure differences due to the experimental programme. However correlations both within individual groups and across all groups were negligible.

---

[1] *Educational Priority, Volume 1: E.P.A. Problems and Policies*, H.M.S.O., 1972, Chapter 7.

Table E.1
Pre-test and post-test scores on the English Picture Vocabulary Test
(Pre-school Version) in the national pre-school experiment, by treatment group

	P.L.D.K. groups		Control groups		Number groups	
	pre-test	post-test	pre-test	post-test	pre-test	post-test
Birmingham groups						
Part-time nursery classes:						
Mean standardized score	94·3	100·1	88·3	96·4	105·5	103·5
Standard deviation	12·9	8·6	16·0	12·1	11·7	10·9
No. of children	18	18	15	15	13	13
Mean age	3y.11m.	4y.7m.	4y.3m.	4y.10m.	3y.6m.	4y.1m.
Full-time nursery classes:						
Mean standardized score	93·8	101·4	94·8	98·6	88·7	94·7
Standard deviation	10·4	8·6	8·8	9·4	15·7	15·4
No. of children	16	16	16	16	15	15
Mean age	4y.1m.	4y.7m.	3y.9m.	4y.4m.	3y.11m.	4y.7m.
Group A playgroups:						
Mean standardized score	97·3	104·4	98·0	100·7	—	—
Standard deviation	10·8	9·1	7·0	8·9	—	—
No. of children	15	15	9	9	—	—
Mean age	3y.9m.	4y.3m.	3y.7m.	4y.1m.	—	—
Group B playgroups:						
Mean standardized score	94·6	99·1	91·4	90·1	88·4	93·4
Standard deviation	6·8	10·1	8·2	17·0	11·8	12·9
No. of children	18	18	14	14	16	16
Mean age	3y.10m.	4y.5m.	3y.8m.	4y.2m.	3y.11m.	4y.5m.
Liverpool and West Riding groups						
Part-time nursery classes:						
Mean standardized score	96·7	98·6	97·9	100·6	—	—
Standard deviation	9·7	13·8	6·8	8·8	—	—
No. of children	21	21	14	14	—	—
Mean age	3y.11m.	4y.8m.	3y.11m.	4y.6m.	—	—
Full-time nursery classes:						
Mean standardized score	83·5	89·4	93·8	93·1	—	—
Standard deviation	14·9	10·9	12·2	10·7	—	—
No. of children	23	23	19	19	—	—
Mean age	3y.9m.	4y.4m.	3y.11m.	4y.5m.	—	—
Playgroups:						
Mean standardized score	102·6	105·7	91·2	95·9	—	—
Standard deviation	11·4	11·8	15·9	12·5	—	—
No. of children	17	17	11	11	—	—
Mean age	3y.9m.	4y.3m.	3y.9m.	4y.6m.	—	—

Table E.2
Pre-test and post-test scores on the Expressive Language Scale of the Reynell Developmental Language Scales in the national pre-school experiment, by treatment group

	P.L.D.K. groups		Control groups		Number groups	
	pre-test	post-test	pre-test	post-test	pre-test	post-test
Birmingham groups						
Part-time nursery classes:						
Mean standardized score	−1·14	−0·09	−1·35	0·10	−1·25	−0·82
Standard deviation	0·87	1·11	1·19	1·02	0·92	0·79
No. of children	13	13	13	13	16	16
Mean age	4y.0m.	4y.7m.	4y.3m.	4y.10m.	3y.5m.	4y.1m.
Full-time nursery classes:						
Mean standardized score	−1·77	−0·01	−0·96	−0·27	−1·45	−0·69
Standard deviation	0·94	1·02	1·10	0·86	1·39	1·14
No. of children	14	14	17	17	15	15
Mean age	4y.1m.	4y.7m.	3y.8m.	4y.4m.	4y.0m.	4y.7m.
Group A playgroups:						
Mean standardized score	−0·70	0·53	−0·71	−0·38	—	—
Standard deviation	1·44	1·03	1·43	1·10	—	—
No. of children	15	15	9	9	—	—
Mean age	3y.9m.	4y.3m.	3y.6m.	4y.1m.	—	—
Group B playgroups:						
Mean standardized score	0·13	1·09	−0·84	−1·07	−0·64	0·06
Standard deviation	1·20	0·74	1·17	1·29	1·16	1·30
No. of children	12	12	12	12	12	12
Mean age	3y.8m.	4y.3m.	3y.9m.	4y.2m.	4y.0m.	4y.6m.
Liverpool and West Riding groups						
Part-time nursery classes:						
Mean standardized score	−0·79	−0·82	0·65	0·23	—	—
Standard deviation	1·08	0·98	0·91	0·61	—	—
No. of children	21	21	14	14	—	—
Mean age	3y.11m.	4y.8m.	3y.11m.	4y.6m.	—	—
Full-time nursery classes:						
Mean standardized score	−1·15	−0·69	0·12	−0·24	—	—
Standard deviation	1·04	0·78	1·11	1·14	—	—
No. of children	23	23	20	20	—	—
Mean age	3y.8m.	4y.4m.	3y.10m.	4y.5m.	—	—
Playgroups:						
Mean standardized score	0·66	0·07	−0·26	0·19	—	—
Standard deviation	1·36	1·12	1·30	0·83	—	—
No. of children	16	16	16	16	—	—
Mean age	3y.10m.	4y.3m.	3y.11m.	4y.6m.	—	—

Table E.3

Pre-test and post-test scores on the Verbal Comprehension Scale of the Reynell Developmental Language Scales in the national pre-school experiment, by treatment group

	P.L.D.K. groups		Control groups		Number groups	
	pre-test	post-test	pre-test	post-test	pre-test	post-test
Birmingham groups						
Part-time nursery classes:						
Mean standardized score	−0·34	0·72	−1·30	−0·31	−0·01	0·13*
Standard deviation	1·56	0·93	1·45	1·44	1·41	1·26
No. of children	13	13	17	17	16	16
Mean age	4y.0m.	4y.7m.	4y.3m.	4y.10m.	3y.5m.	4y.1m.
Full-time nursery classes:						
Mean standardized score	−0·46	0·67	−0·35	0·18	−1·47	−0·36
Standard deviation	1·17	0·72	1·19	0·85	1·56	·1·09
No. of children	14	14	17	17	15	15
Mean age	4y.1m.	4y.7m.	3y.8m.	4y.4m.	4y.0m.	4y.7m.
Group A playgroups:						
Mean standardized score	−0·05	0·62	0·16	0·10	—	—
Standard deviation	1·60	1·14	1·03	0·73	—	—
No. of children	15	15	9	9	—	—
Mean age	3y.9m.	4y.3m.	3y.6m.	4y.1m.	—	—
Group B playgroups:						
Mean standardized score	0·36	0·84	−0·58	−0·26	−0·24	0·12
Standard deviation	0·73	0·39	1·20	1·14	1·18	1·20
No. of children	12	12	13	13	12	12
Mean age	3y.8m.	4y.3m.	3y.9m.	4y.2m.	4y.0m.	4y.6m.
Liverpool and West Riding groups						
Part-time nursery classes:						
Mean standardized score	−0·80	−0·44	1·19	1·04	—	—
Standard deviation	1·05	1·15	0·62	0·58	—	—
No. of children	21	21	14	14	—	—
Mean age	3y.11m.	4y.8m.	3y.11m.	4y.6m.	—	—
Full-time nursery classes:						
Mean standardized score	−1·54	−1·41	0·26	−0·33*	—	—
Standard deviation	1·22	1·03	1·31	1·40	—	—
No. of children	23	23	20	20	—	—
Mean age	3y.8m.	4y.4m.	3y.10m.	4y.5m.	—	—
Playgroups:						
Mean standardized score	0·14	0·43	−0·27	0·25	—	—
Standard deviation	1·19	1·33	1·27	1·06	—	—
No. of children	16	16	16	16	—	—
Mean age	3y.10m.	4y.3m.	3y.11m.	4y.6m.	—	—

Note: * indicates a significant difference favouring the P.L.D.K. group in the amount of improvement between the pre-test and the post-test.

Printed in England for Her Majesty's Stationery Office by McCorquodale (Printers) Limited.
HM 6694 Dd 506677 K30 8 74